FLOORING PSYCH

HOW TO AVOID (LITERALLY)
SLIPPING AND TRIPPING THROUGH LIFE

BARBARA LYONS STEWART, AIA, EDAC

Architectural Design Psychology Press
San Anselmo, CA

Copyright © 2015 by Barbara Lyons Stewart

All rights reserved. No part of this publication may be reproduced, distributed or transmitted in any form or by any means, including photocopying, recording, or other electronic or mechanical methods, without the prior written permission of the publisher, except in the case of brief quotations embodied in critical reviews and certain other noncommercial uses permitted by copyright law. For permission requests, write to the publisher at the address below.

Architectural Design Psychology Press
San Anselmo, California, 94960
Barbara@LyonsArch.com
www.ArchitecturalDesignPsychology.com

Book and E-Book Layout ©2013 BookDesignTemplates.com
Book Cover by BookCoverCafe.com
Photograph on the cover by Sergey Minaev – Fotolia.com

Ordering Information:
Quantity sales. Special discounts are available on quantity purchases by corporations, associations, and others. For details, contact Sales@LyonsArch.com.

Flooring Psych / Barbara Lyons Stewart — March 2015
ISBN   978-0-9904182-1-4

TESTIMONIALS

"<u>Flooring Psych</u> is a quick and enjoyable read. It's also a great reference when considering floor patterns and materials – and their affect on the spaces we design. As designers and architects believing that design makes a difference, we often focus on the delight of the visual and forget the reality of the physical. Barbara's book reinforces the idea that we are responsible for understanding how our designs will affect others."
  Lauren Rottet, FAIA, FIIDA, Rottet Studio,
    Interior Design Hall of Fame, Interiors (now CONTRACT) Designer of the Year

"I appreciate the quotes from my book, <u>Healing Spaces: The Science of Place and Wellbeing</u>, and the way that Barbara has translated my concepts into architectural practice. It is very rewarding to see hypothetical proposals be applied to practice in the real world."
  Esther Sternberg, MD, Research Director, Arizona Center for Integrative Medicine

"AECOM has consulted with Barbara Lyons on three major medical centers. She has worked with our design teams to apply her nature-based environmental psychology research into wonderfully successful outcomes with each project. We have effectively applied the concepts described in her new book, <u>Flooring Psych,</u> and feel that the time spent with Barbara has enhanced how we think as architects, or more importantly, how we can stop thinking like architects for a period and take on the viewpoint of the real end users and people who occupy these spaces."
  Thomas Thompson, Associate Principal and Healthcare Studio Leader, AECOM

"I am honored to have been quoted and agree that feelings and magic are worthy of our attention. The book is well written and beautifully illustrated. I learned a lot."
  Derek Parker, FAIA, RIBA, Fellow of the American College of Healthcare Architects

"We spend our days on floors – walking on them, looking at them, and perched above them – and in this book, Barbara Lyons Stewart helps us do something that no one else has: helping us actually see them and understand the myriad psychological as well as physical aspects of these surfaces, which we occupy most of our lives. This book takes a very human-centered approach to the question of what kind of environments do we want to inhabit and what can we learn not only from modern psychology, but also from ancient wisdom traditions like Vastu Shastra and Geomancy that represented earlier forms of environmental psychology. After reading this book, you will never look at floors – or interior environments – the same way again."

Thomas Fisher, Dean of the College of Design, University of Minnesota

"Flooring Psych is a strong, straightforward read on how best to incorporate flooring – the right flooring – into commercial projects. Architects and Interior Designers will find Barbara's focus on the psychology behind flooring products both useful and entertaining. Flooring manufacturers, dealers, distributors and installers will use this book to educate their clients on the best type, most effective, and appropriate installations of commercial flooring."

Richard N. Pollack, FAIA, FIIDA

"I just finished this book and I LOVED IT! I wish I had read this 30 years ago...and believe it should be required reading for ALL Design Professionals as well as Flooring Manufacturer's sales teams. I will purchase them and hand them out to all my good friends in the business."

Mike Patton, CEO, DSB+ Commercial Floor Finishes, San Francisco Bay Area

"This book has a lot great practical information that will benefit designers who are interested in designing for human health. The content is easy to read, understand, and put into practice. To the author's credit, she stays away from complicated terms, and still manages to convey practical information related to human biology, psychology, and physics within the design process. Flooring Psych has such strong practical value that it is now being used in the Environment and Behavior Studio-Lab at the Boston Architectural College's Masters of Design Studies in Design for Human Health."

Dak Kopec, Ph.D., MS.Arch., MCHES, Director, Masters of Design Studies in Design for Human Health, The Boston Architectural College | School of Design Studies

CONTENTS

FOREWORD 1

INTRODUCTION 5

HOW TO "SEE" YOUR FLOOR PATTERN THE SAME WAY YOUR CLIENTS DO

#1   Our First Impression of Places and Faces 27

HOW TO HELP END-USERS AVOID TRIPPING AND FALLING

#2   "Light is Up" and "Grounding is Good" 45
#3   A Line on the Ground = A Change in Plane 61
#4   Don't Step into the Shadows 73
#5   A Wind Tunnel isn't a Safe Place for People 89

HOW TO HELP PEOPLE GET WHERE THEY WANT TO GO (WAYFINDING)

#6   Organic isn't just a Food Label - We like following a Meandering Path 105
#7   Brains and Feet are Related (Pathways and Landmarks) 119

HOW FLOORING AFFECTS MOOD, BEHAVIOR, CREATIVITY & PRODUCTIVITY

#8   Yin/Yang is the Goldilocks Principle: Too much? Too little? Just right? ... 135

FLOORING AND NATURE – BACK TO THE BASICS

#9   People need Natural Habitats too 165

SUMMARY: How to use these Messages to Benefit your Practice 185
BIBLIOGRAPHY 191
INDEX 199
ABOUT THE AUTHOR 209

iv

*This book is dedicated to Cate, Zach and Doyle
for the love and joy they add to my life,
and to Mary for cheering me along my journey
into the world of flooring.*

This book is written for Architects and Interior Designers because theirs is the world I know and love, although everyone involved in the Flooring Community will find these Hidden Messages interesting and applicable:

- Readers involved in Sales will learn ideas that will give you a new vocabulary to help your own clients select the healthiest colors and patterns for their homes and workplaces.
- Readers involved in Product Design, Research & Development will have a better understanding about the psychological and behavioral role your products will play in the larger design context.
- Flooring Marketers and Manufacturer's Representatives will learn more about the design process and will better understand the issues affecting your designer-clients.
- Building Owners and Facility Managers will learn that the appropriate flooring can promote your personal, professional and financial purposes while reducing tripping and falling incidents.

And you will all discover (like I did) that your flooring design decisions are much more important than you ever believed them to be.

Whether people are fully conscious of this or not, they actually derive countenance and sustenance from the "atmosphere" of the things they live in or with. They are rooted in them just as a plant is in the soil in which it is planted.
   Frank Lloyd Wright

FOREWORD

by Sally Augustin, PhD

Flooring Psych is a rare and useful book. Its straightforward text bridges the chasm between science and design, making it clear that space users benefit when scientists and designers work together.

Environmental psychologists and other social and physical scientists have been actively researching how aspects of the physical environment influence human thought, behavior and wellbeing, for many decades. Most of their research languishes in arcane journals and is never introduced to design practitioners who can use it to enhance lives lived.

Lyons Stewart has carefully reviewed potentially useful studies and translated the ones that designers can apply in practice from "science-ease" into everyday language. Insights from traditional philosophies consistent with these findings are also shared, and they enliven the text.

As I have learned in my own consulting practice, applying the type of information presented in *Flooring Psych* does not restrict a design practitioner's options. Study findings inform the selection of design elements that will be successful in a particular context without mandating that one particular option be selected.

Evidence-Based design research is already part of accepted practice in healthcare and senior living design and material gathered in these environments has been effectively applied in others.

The concepts in this book derived from research in other project types are less known and also supply information that can be applied not only in the sorts of environments where the research was done, but in other locations—educational, retail, corporate, residential, etc.

This comprehensive text is not only practical, but also thought provoking. Readers get the immediate benefit of the material synthesized in the text and are also introduced to a way of thinking and resolving design issues that they can apply throughout their career. It teaches that insights gleaned from scientific studies can improve the world and enhance practice.

Science-informed design also creates a point of competitive differentiation for practitioners. This is particularly important as other professionals, such as facilities and construction managers are beginning to provide services traditionally performed by designers.

Spaces developed using material in this text will not only improve the lives of current space users, but will also better the health of our planet. Spaces that satisfy our most fundamental needs as human beings are less likely to be changed; they already "feel good." This reduces our society's consumption of energy, material, and other resources.

Flooring Psych provides a strong "information foundation" to inform floor-related decisions. It also introduces readers to an important way of thinking about the worlds they live in and design.

Sally Augustin, PhD, MBA, is a practicing environmental psychologist, an author, speaker, consultant and an internationally recognized expert on person-centered design. She is a principal at Design With Science and the editor of Research Design Connections, a science-based design blog read by thousands of individuals each month. Augustin is the president-elect and a Fellow of the American Psychological Association, and also holds leadership positions in other professional organizations including the International Association of Applied Psychology and the Environmental Design Research Association (EDRA).

INTRODUCTION

This book will help you make flooring decisions that will create healthier places whether you are an architect, designer, landscaper, market or sell flooring for a manufacturer, manage facilities for a corporation or are just trying to figure out what flooring to put in your Family Room that will calm down your hyper kids (or rev-up your zoned-out-TV-watching husband).

My reason for writing this book - the first in a series of Architectural Design Psychology books - is to provide timeless research-based recommendations that anyone can use to design supportive spaces more in sync with the goals of our clients and end-users (like healing and productivity) than we are presently doing. I'm starting with floor patterns since flooring is an important feature in every project type. We spend much of our lives walking from place to place; yet we aren't aware of the messages we unconsciously receive from floor patterns with every step we take.

Important Note before you read further:
When I say "floor patterns" I generally mean the large patterns that designers create by combining a variety of different colors and styles in carpet and hard surfaces (rubber, vinyl, LTV, linoleum, ceramic and porcelain tile, stone, hardwood, plastic laminate, terrazzo and every type of paving material) in one

room, corridor or area. I'm not talking about the design of <u>one</u> ceramic, vinyl or carpet tile, for example, although each of those may contain a variety of colors and patterns that contribute to the overall pattern. You'll need to apply the Squint Test to these overall patterns (described by the co-author of my first book) to understand the Hidden Messages described in the following chapters.

> The Squint Test is a technique for ascertaining the impact that visual images have on the subconscious. By closing your eyes to a slit, you no longer see objects as identifiable conscious images but instead perceive only the color contrasts and patterns. This underlying image impacts the subconscious and creates a sense of calmness or chaos, or something in between.
> Vincent M. Smith and Barbara Lyons Stewart,
> <u>Feng Shui: A Practical Guide for Architects and Designers</u>

I. "First Do No Harm" (The quotation attributed to Hippocrates as a guide to physicians) is just as applicable to designers

There are two primary ways that our flooring design choices can either hurt or help:

- Floor Patterns can increase or decrease stress.
- Floor Patterns can lead us where we do (or don't) want to go.
- Floor Patterns can foster or hinder slipping and falling.

> *Slip and fall accidents by customers, employees and pedestrians are a nightmare every commercial building owner and facility manager wants to prevent. With 85 percent of workers' compensation claims attributed to slip and fall accidents (1)... contributing to 2 million fall injuries per year (2), there's real cause for care.*
> Interiors & Sources, November 2013
> (1)   Occupational Health & Safety Administration
> (2)   Consumer Product Safety Commission

We know that slippery floors aren't the only cause of slipping, tripping and falling accidents. Floor patterns and colors also play a role. So learning more about the unconscious psychological effects of flooring will help make your projects safer.

> *Slip, trip, and fall (STF) events are the second leading cause of workers' compensation claims in hospitals. In 2010, a total of 12,400 STF events accounted for 21% of all work-related injuries in hospitals requiring at least 1 day away from work.*
> *"Slipping, Tripping and Falling at Work", Disclosures, June 11, 2012*

Technology (whether the ability to create fanciful, complex and colorful carpet, vinyl and linoleum designs; or twisting, turning and toppling-looking high-rise buildings) is pushing us in the direction where we often design because we CAN and not necessarily because we SHOULD.

The international design and construction community is filled with creatively and technically oriented people from art and engineering backgrounds who love progress and novelty. This is leading our profession in a different direction than most of our clients who judge the success of buildings differently than we do.

> *Hard evidence exists that architecture isn't just what... the tastemakers make of it. The average person looks at architecture more with emotion than with intellect..."*
> *Architect Magazine, May 2007*

> *... building preferences are perceived differently by architects and lay critics, even when the architects are asked to think like non-architects.*
> *Brown Graham, Robert Gifford, Journal of Environmental Psychology, 2001*

> *Human physiological and psychological response seldom figures in design discussions today. Architects pretend to have surpassed human nature. Instead, certain formal and abstract notions about space, materials, and form are of primary concern. Those do not arise, however from a full understanding of the processes at work that give human beings their existential foothold on earth.*
> *Nikos Salingaros and Kenneth Masden II in* <u>Biophilic Design</u>

Stress and Design

Stress has been proven to cause depression and disease. Studies from a variety of fields confirm that architectural and interior design features can increase or decrease stress and anxiety.

> *Previous studies have established that a relationship exists between poor housing and psychological distress.*
> *Dunn & Hayes, 2000; Evan, Saltzman, & Cooperman, 2001; Hopton & Hunt, 1996). Informedesign: "Housing Quality Affects Mental Health"*

> *There is abundant evidence indicating that psychological stressors are associated with illness*
> *(Gunderson & Rahe, 1974; Henry, Meehan & Stephens, Weiner, 1977; Rogers, 1979)*

Designing to promote health (and happiness) is largely about reducing stress. We encounter thousands of stressful details each day: from beeping cell phones and innumerable e-mails to traffic jams and road rage. This type of everyday stress is our enemy since our bodies automatically release the chemicals cortisol and adrenaline when we are under stress.

That's not necessarily a bad thing. But the human body developed biologically in the wilderness over hundreds of thousands of years to handle occasional MAJOR stress surges – like when our ancestors were calmly hunting and gathering in the wilderness and someone screamed,

"Here comes the lion! RUNNNNNNNNN!!!!!!"

We're fine with that. But our bodies didn't develop to handle the chronic stress we experience daily. Modern science has confirmed that constant low levels of the stress-hormones cortisol and adrenaline wear down our immune systems. This leaves us open to disease and depression. If you can help reduce stress through your design recommendations and choices, then why wouldn't you do that?

> The daily stresses of the modern world can throw our bodies into emergency mode and keep us there. That takes a toll through high blood pressure, tension headaches and a lot of gnawed pencils.
> "If you're chronically releasing stress hormones, your body starts to fall apart," says University of Virginia neuroscientist James Coan.
> "Ultimately, you're going to live less long – and you're going to be miserable."
> TIME Magazine, January 28, 2008

II. The reasons why designers will want to learn more about Research-Based Design.

> Incorporating research into projects adds credibility and provides a competitive edge to healthcare design practitioners, providers and manufacturers who are aiming to determine the potential and actual impact of planned capital investments in facility design, optimize the healthcare experience, drive patient and performance value, and deliver on critical healthcare performance measurements.
> The Center for Health Design, https://www.healthdesign.org/

There are three trends happening in our profession that will dramatically change the way we design in the future:

Trend #1. Evidence-Based Design (EBD) will spread to other project types from its stronghold in healthcare design.

> An evidence-based designer makes decisions – with an informed client – based on the best available information from credible research and evaluations of projects.
> (Kirk Hamilton, 2005)

There is a <u>huge</u> financial incentive for healthcare organizations to use design as another tool to get people up and out of hospitals ASAP. Anyone who has been in a hospital lately has experienced that uncomfortable reality. Healthcare organizations are my main Architectural Design

Psychology clients since they are more open to the idea that we can change our environment to improve health and performance than other industries. They've seen the results of the exponentially increasing number of Evidence Based Design (EBD) Studies that they want their designers to apply. What you learn in this book will definitely help you attract healthcare clients if that is your goal.

Healthcare design firms know how necessary EBD experience and credentials have become. Since its launch in 2009, more than 1,500 individuals throughout the world have obtained EDAC credentials (Evidence-Based Design Accreditation and Certification) from the Center for Health Design. The CHD also sponsors Healthcare Design Magazine, Healthcare Design Conferences, and dozens of other publications and programs. At the time of this printing, 41 industry organizations and more than 100 design firms endorse Evidence-Based Design.

> *As the body of knowledge grows, we think it's critical that this evidence be applied competently and credibly to build better buildings. Looking forward, EDAC means new and higher expectations from all of us about what we design every day.*
> The Center for Health Design, <u>An Introduction to Evidence-Based Design</u>

Very few healthcare facilities are planned and designed today without incorporating Evidence-Based Design Research relating to:
- Improving building systems, fixtures and materials. (That is definitely NOT the subject of this book, although some of the research studies in these areas are described in the resources noted in the Bibliography).
- Improving the psychological and physical health of people living and working in the spaces we design thru features like flooring.

> *Now there's enough research – peer-reviewed research – for us to know without a shadow of a doubt that the built environment plays a significant role in errors, costs, infections, stress, waste, and satisfaction...*
> Derek Parker, FAIA, RIBA, FACHA, "See: The Potential of Place." 2006

The Benefits of Research to Clients with other Project Types:

Designing buildings based upon function and aesthetics will not be enough when building owners and clients with other project types learn that research exists in multiple disciplines (including EBD) that can help promote their own goals and improve their bottom line by:

- Improving staff retention and satisfaction.
- Reducing staff health problems and absenteeism.
- Increasing end-user and client satisfaction.
- Enhancing productivity, creativity and concentration.

It's feasible that successful design firms in the future in every practice area will have as many staff members with research knowledge as they have with LEED certification (which is just one specific type of research, after all).

> In terms of the practice evolution of architecture, Potter called for architects to spend more time making the empirical case for design value to their clients and communities. "Architects have a robust culture of aesthetics, but we don't have a very strong culture in the syntax of proof," he said. "Each day, more and more data is uncovered detailing how well-designed office space can increase worker productivity, and how quality healthcare environments can augment healing and decrease hospital stays."
> Jeffrey Potter, AIA 2012 National President, AIA 2012 Institute Update

SIDENOTE:

I can attest to the success of discussing research-based design with potential clients. Amazingly, I win most of the corporate architecture/interior design projects I interview for (against firms of 100 people in some cases). The only project I lost in the past six years went to the best friend of the client's brother. My clients select me because I question them about their professional goals during the interview and suggest ways that our design could reinforce the best end-user behavior to support their needs. I don't focus on aesthetics (which is a subjective grey area to most clients) or function. They assume I'm competent at both or I wouldn't have been short-listed.

Trend #2. The project responsibilities of architects may increase if we can promote our clients' goals more effectively.

> *As pre-design, management and construction consultants nibble away at the tasks previously controlled by architects, the role of the architect has been described as diminishing... Many architects are thought to be subjective proponents of aesthetics when the client is interested in efficiency and performance...*
> D. Kirk Hamilton and David H. Watkins,
> <u>Evidence Based Design for Multiple Business Types</u>

Professional associations like the American Institute of Architects are concerned with the decreasing perceived importance of design-professionals in the eyes of clients who sometimes rely on architects primarily for design expertise and construction document preparation.

However, the research-based design benefits listed above translate into major client ROI (Return on Investment). Only design professionals have the talents, skill-sets and access to effectively incorporate research into the design process. That's not something construction managers or contractors can do.

While research specialists have a role to play, in my experience very few understand the exact timing when specific studies must be applied to design decision-making (or when "that ship has sailed" and recommendations would lengthen the schedule or increase project costs). That understanding has been critical to my success as an Architectural Design Psychology Consultant on large project teams – and it will help you too!

When design professionals are recognized as important advocates in promoting the financial and business success of clients, then they won't be "line items" on the project budget.

Trend #3. Environmental concerns and sustainability practices are leading us back to understanding that the health of People and of the Planet are one and the same thing.

> *For human survival and mental health and fulfillment, we need the natural setting in which the human mind almost certainly evolved and in which culture has developed over these millions of years of evolution.*
> E.O Wilson, "Arousing Biophilia"

I often hear in seminars and at conferences how frustrated architects and designers feel when they want to incorporate nature-based and sustainable features into their projects (like water retention systems, green roofs and walls, etc.) but their clients can't even consider these features due to budget constraints. The concepts described in this book could be termed "Psychological Sustainability" features since they are equally nature-based. They also contribute to the longevity of buildings by creating places people find nurturing and supportive – and will want to maintain. These nature-based strategies do not increase costs and can often <u>save</u> the client money. You will read MUCH more about the people and planet connection in the following Hidden Message chapters.

III. How do you start incorporating research?

And who has the time to do research anyway?

What do you do if your firm isn't large enough to hire a research specialist? And you're still learning BIM and can't add ONE MORE THING to your schedule? Well, read on, because the Architectural Design Psychology approach is an easily learned and remembered way to incorporate research into your design process.

The Center for Health Design has identified eight levels of rigor to identify the way architects and designers can incorporate Evidence Based Design within their practices.

The Architectural Design Psychology approach meets the first two:
  #1   Define Evidence-Based Design Goals and Objectives
  #2   Find Sources for Relevant Experience

This system doesn't include conducting and evaluating your own research studies. But it's a good beginning.

In this book you will learn a simple framework for applying research to floor pattern design. Instead of trying to remember and prioritize hundreds of studies, you can evaluate any flooring design decision by deciding which of the 9 Hidden Messages are most applicable to your client's specific goals and project.

What is the Architectural Design Psychology Approach?

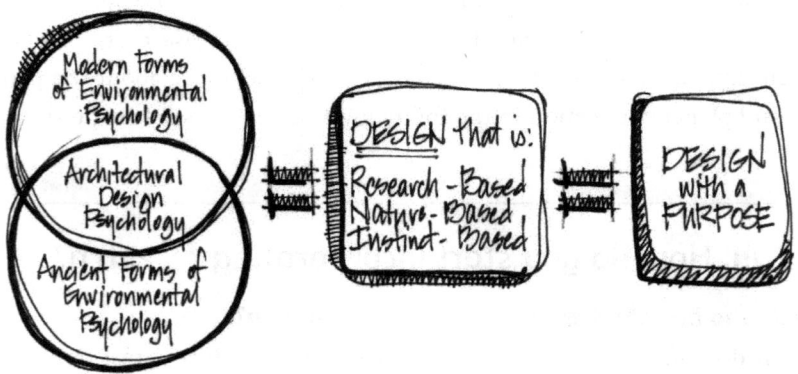

Like designers everywhere, I always knew that places could affect us psychologically – but not how or why.

> *It is a matter of common observation that the moods of men are changed by environment, by ugliness and beauty, by sunny weather and rainy weather... Placed in a bright harmonious setting, most people will find their dispositions improved.*
> Faber Birren, <u>Color Psychology and Color Therapy</u>

But what defines a "bright harmonious setting" and how can we design to achieve specific goals like productivity or concentration? That isn't a part of a typical architectural education. After earning a Masters in Architecture from the University of Minnesota in chilly Minneapolis, I worked at Ellerbe and RSP in Minneapolis, SOM in Chicago and then moved to San Francisco to switch into Interior Architecture and later start my firm, Lyons Stewart Architects. In my free time, I read whatever I could find that linked the environment with human behavior.

There wasn't much information in the architectural world until the past few years but other disciplines were producing research studies providing clues to how design affects people.

These are a just a few of the areas producing current research:

Modern Scientific Disciplines Linking People and Places

Environmental Psychology	Biophilia
Psychology	Applied Psychology
Ecological Psychology	Evolutionary Psychology
Human Ecology	Evolutionary Biology
Research in Color	Research in Lighting
Evidence-Based Design	Neuroscience

These fields have produced thousands of studies. So I kept reading books and online references thinking:
"I can use this idea... and this one.... and this one..."

Until I came to the end of each book and whined,
"No way! How can I use hundreds of ideas when I only have two weeks for schematic design?
What should my priorities be?
Christopher Alexander's book Pattern Language *has 383 patterns!*
Dak Kopec's book Environmental Psychology for Design *and Sally Augustin's book* Place Advantage *describe thousands of scientific studies!"*

Those are just three experts with valuable design-related research. What should I do first? And how could I juggle variables like culture, climate, age and project type? It seemed overwhelming.

I needed the CliffsNotes version...

Well, (I reasoned) if I were designing a zoo enclosure for the large apes with whom we share 98.4% of our DNA (think about that statistic) then I would definitely research their natural habitat in Africa in order to design an environment where apes would be happiest and healthiest. Why would OUR natural habitat be any less important to OUR health? (Although studies show that most people don't believe that the rules applying to animals may also apply to people).

> *Interactional Theory... declares that people and the environment are separate entities that constantly interact.*
> *Transactional Theory... contends that the human-environment relationship is mutually supportive.*
> *Ironically, humans seem to have little difficulty understanding the Transactional relationship between the environment and other life forms, but when it comes to their own species, most cling to an Interactional perspective.*
>   Dak Kopec, Environmental Psychology for Design

Brainstorm #1! Since I believed in the importance of focusing on people's natural habitats, then research describing design ideas coming directly from NATURE needed to be one "CliffsNotes Limiter".

> *Like those of other living things, our structure, development and behavior rise from a genetic foundation sunk in an environmental context. Yet while we readily accept that a healthy seed can't grow into a plant without the right soil, light, and water and that a feral dog won't behave like a pet, we resist recognizing the importance of environment in our own lives...but place is important to human beings right from the beginning...*
>   Myron Hofer, The Roots of Human Behavior

Nature and Human Instinct: Back to the Basics

Then, I asked myself (always trying to simplify ideas to the point where I could actually USE them in the design process - next week),

"What besides natural habitat would determine how healthy and happy people are in a specific environment? What universal concepts transcend culture, age, climate and project type?"

My answer, *"Human Instincts like 'Fight or Flight'."*

> *Instinct, then, is essentially that part of our behavior, which is not learned.*
> Robert Winston, Human Instinct

The Fight or Flight instinct describes our unconscious and conscious need to protect ourselves. Ask anyone who has seen old Mafia movies where the Don sits in an Italian Restaurant and you'll hear:

"The Mafia Don sits in the far corner, back to the wall, with a view of the door."

That's defensive positioning and human instinct. Environmental Psychologists call this concept the Prospect and Refuge Theory. It is part of the Savannah Hypothesis explained by the proven-by-DNA fact that all our ancestors came from the same African tribe before leaving Africa at 20,000-year intervals to populate the planet.

The safest place on the savannah was on a small hill with a tree overlooking the grasslands. The hill provided "prospect" allowing people to see predators advancing in the grass, and "refuge" since it masked our ancestor's silhouette and allowed a place to climb if a big-toothed animal approached. The tree gave our ancestors the same back protection beloved by Mafia Dons.

This human instinct influences the standard default locations for beds, chairs and desks inside rooms (although we may not consciously recognize that fact while we're laying out furniture on Space Plans). Neuroscientists say that our brains haven't changed much since our ancestors walked out of Africa about 100,000 years ago. In many ways we instinctively respond to our modern-built environments the same way our ancient relatives responded to their natural environments.

> *We are all Stone-agers living in the fast lane.*
> *Evolutionary Biology*

How could I find other instinct-related design ideas? I thought that ancient building practices would provide a bridge to the past. Any design ideas that have lasted thousands of years must reinforce human instinct or they would have been replaced by an ever-changing series of "better" ideas (like the architectural styles that have continuously replaced other architectural styles in the past 150 years).

> *Traditions are the guideposts driven deep in our subconscious minds. The most powerful ones are those we can't even describe, aren't even aware of.*
> Ellen Goodman

Ancient Building Design Practices Linking People and Places

So I jumped into the world of Ancient Philosophies of Environmental Psychology including Vastu Shastra from India (5,000 years old) and Feng Shui from China (4,000 years old). I learned that one of the primary principles in Feng Shui is the Commanding Position.

This concept was used to locate farmhouses on a property with a mountain to the back for protection from the elements and marauders, a hill or high trees on each side, and open vistas to the front for sunlight, crop viewing and inspiration. The Commanding Position is just another (and much older) interpretation of the Prospect and Refuge Theory.

Then I learned that all ancient cultures from Ireland to Australia and Africa to the Americas, developed their own similar life-nurturing building design practices. These were all based upon the earth sciences collectively called Geomancy (derived from "Gaia", the Greek name for the Earth Goddess). Unfortunately, most cultures didn't document their practices as well as the ancient Chinese and Indians did.

> *Wilson has... provided a biological basis for what was previously attributed to the supernatural aspects of human nature (Wilson 1978, 1984)... We are finally accumulating scientific evidence to support conclusions reached much earlier by traditional societies.*
> Nikos Salingaros and Kenneth Masden II in <u>Biophilic Design</u>

Following this path, I became a Certified Feng Shui Practitioner and eventually co-authored a book with Vincent Smith as part of Kaplan's Professional Management Series for Architects and Engineers named <u>Feng Shui: A Practical Guide for Architects and Designers</u>.

> *Despite its pragmatic aspects, feng shui is in a sense a Rosetta Stone linking man and his environment, ancient ways and modern life... Feng Shui is the key to understanding the silent dialogue between man and nature, whispered through the cosmic breath, spirit – ch'i.*
> Sarah Rossbach, <u>Feng Shui: The Chinese Art of Placement</u>

Abandoning my architectural practice to be a Feng Shui consultant was never my intention. My goal has always been to find the kernels of truth in ancient building practices. Since these have been handed down for thousands of years (I reasoned) they must be based upon human instinct and would be equally relevant today.

What did I learn was the most important building design concept shared by Feng Shui, Vastu Shastra and <u>every</u> ancient culture in both icy and scorching climates?

Ancient cultures all over the world believed their survival depended upon following the laws of Nature in how they lived their lives – and in how they built their buildings.

Our ancestors believed that if their buildings were designed in sync with the natural world (its patterns, relationships, cycles and energies) then they, their families, and their communities would be more likely to prosper – because weren't people just another part of the Circle of Life?

> *In the Circle, we are all equal. When in the Circle, no one is in front of you. No one is behind you. No one is above you. No one is below you. The Sacred Circle is designed to create unity... there is a place for every species, every race, every tree and every plant. It is this completeness of Life that must be respected in order to bring about health on this planet.*
>   Dave Chief, Oglala Lakota

> *When we surround ourselves with nature and let it take us deep within ourselves, we experience inner calm... and we can learn the truth in the Vedic message "Thou Art That."*
>   Kathleen Cox, The Power of Vastu Living

> *Regarding the physiological effects of nature exposure, restoration is apparent when changes in bodily systems indicate decreased stress mobilization (for instance, reduced sympathetic nervous system activity). Physiological restoration is manifest within 3 minutes at most, or as fast as a few seconds in certain systems.*
>   (Fredrickson and Levenson, 1998: Hartig, Evans, Jamner, Davis and Garling, 2003) HERD, Spring 2008 Vol.1

18 Instinct-Based Design Principles – My Framework

I combined research from both ancient and modern forms of Environmental Psychology, kept simplifying and simplifying; looking for the "big" ideas that transcended time and design styles. I finally ended up with 18 Instinct-Based Design Principles that I organized into a 3-Part System I could use as a consultant on any project.

(If you would like to learn more about these 18 Principles and how to apply them to other architectural and interior design features besides flooring, then please visit the website www. ArchitecturalDesignPsychology. com).

The most significant and simple ideas about the importance of nature and human instinct came from ancient sources since science agrees that our minds haven't changed much over time. But I only considered ancient design concepts valid if they were confirmed by multiple modern scientific studies developed by experts from a variety of fields.

> *Around 100,000 years ago, some of our ancestors began to emigrate out of Africa, and eventually colonized the whole world. But 100,000 years is only about 8,000 generations – too short a time for evolution to produce any major changes. Humans haven't changed much in that time, so we can ignore it when discussing the evolution of the mind.*
> Dylan Evans and Oscar Zarate, <u>Introducing Evolutionary Psychology</u>

In all honesty, professional researchers don't follow this process. I am not a research specialist. I find research studies and theories that make sense to me after decades of design experience and observation. I translate that information into practical design strategies that architects and interior designers can apply to any project TOMORROW.

My role is to be an interpreter only. I am in awe of - and I thank - the research specialists who developed the studies that have informed my process, especially those whom I have quoted in this book.

The Relationship between Floor Patterns and Human Instinct

In 2011, I gave a seminar at the Healthcare Design Conference in Nashville titled *Flooring Patterns in Healthcare Facilities: Friend or Foe?* I had looked through my 18 Principles, and found that more related in some way to flooring than to any other design feature. I also described a few of these principles in seminars at the 2012 National AIA Conference and to Southern California IIDA Chapters in 2012 in their annual Speaker Series.

The importance of floor patterns makes total sense when you think that our ancient ancestors were constantly looking at the ground. Ground features were critically important to their health and survival. In a world without antibiotics and orthopedic surgeons, tripping and falling could mean sitting under a tree with a broken leg while watching your Clan file off into the distance as they followed the buffalo.

> *Through evolution we have tuned our attentional system to be more sensitive to objects in our lower visual field... since our ancestors were more likely to find tracks of prey and lurking predators on the ground and in bushes than up in the trees.*
> *(Gazzaniga, 1998)*

Why do I call these Flooring Concepts "Hidden Messages"?

I call them "Hidden Messages" because most architects and designers never learned floor pattern psychology in school or in practice.

Additionally, most design professionals are not aware that clients experience space very differently than we do. So what is in plain view to end-users is still hidden to designers (and vice versa) unless we purposely train our minds to experience space the same way non-designers do. That's what this book will help you do.

> *Along with the basic knowledge we acquire, we seem to learn a 'way of seeing' that is characteristic of our chosen profession... Architects see form, light and color where the rest of us see walls, floors and doors...*
> Robert Gifford, <u>Environmental Psychology Principles and Practice</u>

"Seeing space differently" also applies to everyone in the flooring, facilities management and construction worlds since they have too much specialized knowledge to experience space the way typical occupants would.

We don't see things as they are. We see them as we are.
 Anais Nin

IV. The Architectural Design Psychology Approach is easy to learn when you switch from a Creative Innovation-Based Perspective to an Instinctive Experiential-Based Perspective

The unconscious, as the result of its spatio-temporal relativity, possesses better sources of information than the conscious mind — which has only sense perceptions available to it....
 Carl Jung

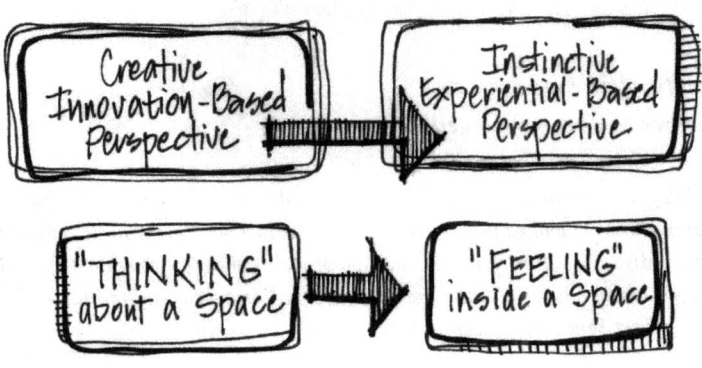

It doesn't take an advanced degree in Shamanism to move architecture... It begins simply with opening our hearts, letting go of the intellectual, verbal and physical noise of our culture, and listening to what is really needed in everything we design.
 Tom Bender in <u>Biophilic Design</u>

Before you begin reading the Hidden Messages chapters, it is best to internalize two key strategies that will help jumpstart your understanding about how incredibly important floor patterns are to all of us:

#1. Identify your Avatar

When a client asks me to work with his or her project team as a consultant, I often find myself listening to design presentations by architects and interior designers where I start thinking, *"Great design idea...."* and then I realize that I need to mentally shake myself and say,
"No! I'm not here to think like a designer!"
My role is to imagine that I am hot and tired 75-yr-old Ethel from Modesto walking into the clinic with my 80-yr-old obese husband Ed.

Or I am 28-yr-old depressed Sam having a hard time staying motivated and positive at my demanding tech firm sitting at an open table with no privacy, surrounded by competitors and staring at my computer 60 hours a week.

"How does <u>this</u> design alternate make me feel NOW?

More confused or more confident?
More depressed or more energetic?"

> *Sociologist William Deane resided on a mental ward for a week... He observed that the hospital looked very different from the inside: "This is in no sense a perceptual distortion. It is rather a condition of seeing things through a different set of eyes, which has the effect of making the familiar appear unfamiliar."*
> Robert Sommer, <u>Personal Space</u>

For those of you involved in a healthcare project or one involving the elderly or vision-impaired, it is even more important to focus on how a specific design alternate <u>feels</u>, since studies show that the more vulnerable someone is physically and/or psychologically, the more their environment affects them.

Switching your mental perspective isn't difficult, but it takes constant effort since your education and experience have trained you to think differently than your clients (and most of humanity) think.

This is the second tool I use when I review Schematic or Design Development alternates: I ask myself how they could relate to a pattern in nature. Then I force my brain to jump back into the distant past to…

#2. Think like a Caveman (or Cavewoman)

When you look for instinctive Hidden Messages while reviewing design alternates, sometimes it helps to pretend you're Ayla from Clan of the Cave Bear or Conan from Conan the Barbarian, (people who would definitely have felt space instead of intellectualized it). Just keep asking yourself questions, and then answering from their perspective:

"What ground feature in nature is most like this pattern?
Would the ground pattern ahead look safe? Questionable? Dangerous?

Does that shape on the path look like something I'll need to step over?
Or something I might sink into?

Small twigs or a larger branch? A pile of soft leaves? Or an insect nest?
Slippery mud? White ice? Or the dry trampled-down dirt floor in my cave?"

> *Human beings are most comfortable in spaces that capture the essence of our primordial homes.*
>   *(Kellert, 2005)*

> *There is a hardwired set of memories (such as a hearth or garden setting) still accessible in those with Alzheimer's disease that can provide a calming effect.*
>   *John Eberhard, The Academy of Neurosciences for Architecture, 2005*

It isn't difficult to "see" the world as literally as our ancient ancestors did. But if you're having trouble mentally leaping back in time then just pretend you are on the set of a *Survivor* episode – without the cameras. Remember that human instinct has <u>nothing</u> to do with design trends and styles. You can use the concepts described in this book with every design style you can imagine. These nature-based and instinct-based ideas will feel right, will help reduce stress and will cost nothing.

Have fun incorporating these Hidden Messages!

As soon as you read them you will probably think, *"I already know that!"* And you do! But you might not verbalize these ideas when you design or when you teach the next generation of designers. When one of my friends, Doug, became a Partner at Gensler and found himself managing multiple large projects simultaneously, he described walking through a project after construction. He noticed a design flaw that <u>he</u> would never have made as a project designer and said *"How did this happen? This isn't a detail we use!"* Then he realized that he hadn't communicated what <u>he</u> had learned through years of practice to the young project designer.

This book will make you conscious of what many of you do unconsciously, and will help you better communicate your ideas. But most importantly – I hope that the one idea you take from this book is this:

Research confirms that in order to create healthy places, design should be based upon Human Instinct and Nature – instead of Human Ego and Design Fads.

> *Young people, I want to beg of you always keep your eyes open to what Mother Nature has to teach you. By doing so you will learn many valuable things every day of your life.*
> George Washington Carver

HIDDEN MESSAGE #1:

The First Impression of a Place is as Important as the First Impression of a Face

> *It is only shallow people who do not judge by appearances.*
> Oscar Wilde (1854 - 1900)

> *Our first view of a space has a significant influence on how information about that space is stored. A recent study has found that this first impression is used to organize that data about the space in long-term memory.*
> Kelly, Avaamides and Loomis, Journal of Experimental Psychology, 2007

IN THIS CHAPTER YOU WILL LEARN:
- HOW FLOORING CONTRIBUTES TO FIRST IMPRESSIONS.
- HOW "MIRRORING" OCCURS AT HOME AND WORK.
- HOW CHANGING THE ENVIRONMENT CAN CHANGE LIVES.

It is appropriate that the first concept in this book relates to First Impressions. We experience First Impressions hundreds of times each day (every time we walk through a doorway or around a corner). We generally don't realize that they are based upon our subconscious thoughts and instincts or how much they affect our daily expectations and behavior.

> *Of our sensory organs, none is more active than our eyes. The nervous system will use billions of receptors to process information; almost two-thirds of these are related to vision... a picture is truly worth a thousand words. And your first impression may very well be most of the story.*
> William Spear, <u>Feng Shui Made Easy</u>

I. The Importance of the First Impression: "What you see is what you get"

> *Research links attractiveness with patient satisfaction and perceived quality of care, so flooring selected must appeal to the population being served.*
> (Becker, 2008)

> *Boosting curb appeal is one investment you're almost guaranteed to recoup.*
> National Association of Realtors

First Impressions aren't just about viewing buildings from the outside. One of the most important First Impressions occurs when we step into a building or space through the main entrance. We instinctively make a mental transition from "outside" to "inside" and from "public" to "private". In his influential book <u>Pattern Language</u>, architect Christopher Alexander named this area the Entrance Transition.

> *Pattern #112   Entrance Transition*
> *The experience of entering a building influences the way you feel inside the building. If the transition is too abrupt there is no feeling of arrival, and the inside of the building fails to be an inner sanctum.*
> Christopher Alexander, <u>Pattern Language</u>

Builders throughout history recognized that the flooring in this Entrance Transition area contributes substantially to our expectations and knowledge about the people inside the building.

> *The arrangements of spaces should clearly define territorial and spatial hierarchies within the building...Transition zones are particularly important: hallways, doorway alcoves, and so on.*
> Andrew Baum and Jerome Singer, <u>Advances in Environmental Psychology</u>

Examples of Purposely Designed First Impressions

- The monumental entry halls in the government buildings that Albert Speer designed for Adolph Hitler with dramatic marble flooring, columns and walls purposely make people feel insignificant and powerless.

- Traditional Japanese homes often had a special paving guest stone at the public side of the threshold, and a host stone on the private side. Additionally, the Japanese custom of exchanging street shoes for clean and comfortable slippers inside the entrance requires a physical action that sends the message,
"Leave your public face outside. You are entering a private place."

- Churches are typically not entered directly from a busy street but through a series of threshold and vestibule experiences with a variety of floor pattern transitions that reinforce the desired inner spiritual preparation.

- Feng Shui calls the area immediately inside the major entry of every type of building the Min Tang or "Bright Palace" because of the energy shift that occurs here. We can reinforce this shift through design to change expectations and behavior.

> *The progressive move from the real world to the artificial world of the theater can mean passing through a sequence of changing spaces, gradually lowering of lighting, and changes in acoustics and other distractions to remove the audience from the street.*
> D. Kirk Hamilton and David H. Watkins,
> <u>Evidence-Based Design for Multiple Building Types</u>

Sunday Open Houses: First Impressions affect cost (and us)

Everyone who has ever walked into an Open House on a Sunday afternoon knows how easy it is to make assumptions about the sellers. Flooring type and condition are some of the features that help us guess their identities:

- Worn carpet, stained grout between 4x4 ceramic tiles on the bathroom floor, 1970s furniture and fading photographs. *(probably elderly and not doing well financially ?)*

- A West Elm linen-wrapped mattress on a newly polished dark brown wood plank floor, folding chairs, large flat screen TV, immaculate porcelain tile bathroom and kitchen floors *(probably young with a great job but no time to buy furniture or spend time at home – relocating closer to work?)*

> *Research has shown that we can consistently and correctly infer the personality and interests of other people from the material that they present to the world. (Gosling, Ko, Mannarelli, and Morris, 2002)*

An entirely new industry, Staging, has developed for the direct purpose of influencing First Impressions and increasing the perceived value of a home in the eyes of buyers. Staging pays for itself many times over, according to the Real Estate Agents who recommend that service to sellers trying to maximize their profits.

II. You can purposely design Floor Patterns to shift energy at every "entrance"

Shifting energy from Public to Private spaces

Most cultures throughout history have chosen to identify the transition area between public and private spaces of all kinds with a positive message through design features that signal "you have arrived", "you are safe" or "you are home." The obvious residential example is the "Welcome Home" doormat.

In all project types this typically means that flooring materials become softer and more comfortable with smaller patterns as someone transitions from a streetscape deeper into a building interior:

Standard Flooring Transitions in a Corporate Hi-Rise

This typical flooring progression positively reinforces the psychological change our brain experiences moving from public to private space:
- Concrete paving on sidewalks outside, transitioning...
- To a large-scale stone pattern in the Ground Floor Lobby...
- To a smaller-scale stone pattern inside the Elevator Lobby...
- To high quality broadloom carpet inside the Elevator Cab...
- To stone tiles bordering a high quality broadloom carpet on each Multi-Tenant Elevator Lobby...
- To high quality flooring (broadloom, carpet tiles, wood, stone or tile) in the Tenant's Reception Area...
- To lower quality flooring inside the Corporate Space (designed to reinforce the client's specific business goal: professional, tech, healthcare, government etc.)...
- To a variety of flooring types inside private offices and support areas depending upon function (carpet, linoleum, VCT etc.)...
- To 6 x 6 (or smaller) tiles on the Rest Room floors.

Since our design decisions shift the energy of everyone entering space, our clients will benefit if that shift is discussed during Programming. Then the transition zones entering and inside their building can purposely reinforce their preferred image and business goals instead of being just part of an overall design scheme that doesn't incorporate the psychology of their staff and visitors.

Bringing Purpose and Feeling into the Programming Phase

How do your clients <u>want</u> people to feel when they enter?

- Intimidated/impressed or comfortable?
- Traditional or "cutting edge?"
- Professional or unconventional?
- Energetic or relaxed?
- Focused or expansive?
- Creatively challenged or safely nurtured?

You can develop a list of the adjectives that apply to your project type.

<u>None of these choices is good or bad!</u>

The message you want to send to the staff and visitors of your Wall Street Law Firm Client will probably be different than the message you want to send to the staff and visitors of your Silicon Valley Law Firm Client. When you establish your client's goals then you can design to meet those goals while incorporating your own ideas about good design.

> *The (hotel) lobby is the center of guest travel and activity; and, as the first space a person experiences upon entering, its characteristics establish the environment's image (e.g., luxurious, rugged, fantastic). The image sets a mood and ideally will inspire patrons' positive emotions.*
> Dak Kopec, <u>Environmental Psychology for Design</u>

If you are thinking, *"of course the design of those spaces would look different,"* then try to stop thinking about how the design will <u>look</u> (which is extremely difficult for visually-oriented design professionals to do). It helps to identify the best mood and psychological goals of a specific space <u>in your client's own words</u> long before you turn on your "design brain" and begin thinking in images and sketching on napkins, tracing paper, tablets or computers.

The Importance of Verbalizing before Visualizing

When you "use your words first" (Okay, that does sound like what a parent says to an over-active preschooler, but the advice is just as valid for designers), your own subjective design ideas won't trump what would actually be best for your client. It's too easy for creative design professionals to see a fabulous new tile floor product, starchitect-designed chair, sustainable green wall or another compelling design feature in a professional publication or design showroom and want to use it on their very next project.

Visualizing images first often leads to designing from a place of ego instead of service because it takes the focus away from the client's needs and wants.

Reality check:
- Is your primary design goal to be published and win the approval and applause of peers in the design profession?
- Or are you designing the best space for your specific clients who will keep coming back to you and be a great reference because you really listened to what they needed and helped them achieve their business or personal goals through your design expertise?

Sometimes a design can do both – but not always. As the following study shows, incorporating research often blasts away pre-conceived design ideas. But if you do start with words and listening then you are more likely to have a recurring, appreciative client AND a great design.

> *Does Evidence Base Design make designing facilities more difficult?*
>
> *35.29% - EBD helps us quickly and efficiently design quality interior spaces*
> *58.82% - EBD can sometimes contradict our original design, forcing us to rethink the space*
> *5.88% - We rarely, if ever, follow EBD practices consciously*
> *(Healthcare Design Magazine online poll 2.8.2010)*

Question:
- What if you are designing for yourself or your family?
  Or for a client who already knows and loves you?
  Why would identifying First Impressions matter then?

Answer:
- The hundreds of First Impressions we experience daily (including what we see when we walk down the street and walk through every doorway inside a building) add up. People will end their day either crazy-stressed or calm, in some part due to the accumulation of the First Impressions they experienced.

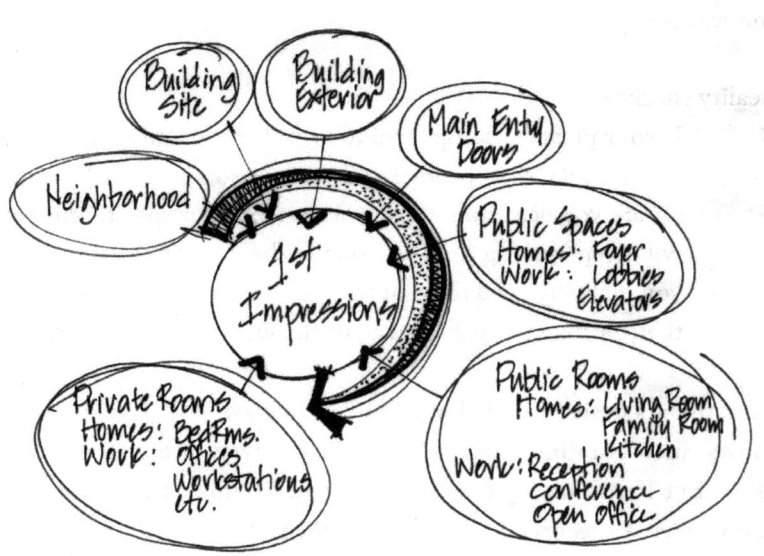

1st Impressions are most important in the places where we spend the majority of our time - in our homes and workplaces.

This leads to a variation of the First Impression Principle:

III. Mirroring is The Architectural Law of Attraction

Throughout history, people have believed that the places where we spend most of our time don't just tell OTHER people about us. The places where we live and work constantly tell us about OURSELVES. Our environment makes us behave and act in specific ways – an unending cycle of "mirroring".

> *We shape our buildings: thereafter they shape us.*
> *Winston Churchill*

> *Transactionalism emphasizes that a person and an environment are part of one inclusive entity. This means that neither individuals nor settings can be adequately defined without reference to the other and that activities of one necessarily influence the other. We influence environments and environments influence us.*
> *Robert Gifford, Environmental Psychology Principles and Practice*

> *Living in a crooked house will make your life full of crooked things. Because who you are, the way you perceive your life, and what's going on now will be revealed in your environment.*
> *William Spear, Feng Shui Made Easy*

Ancient Chinese and Indian traditions (and modern quantum physics) teach that our human energy interacts with the energy of our immediate environment: molecules engaged in a constant dance.

This energy dance (mirroring) means that we need to think very carefully about the design of the places where we live and work (including floors, walls, finishes and furniture) because the combination of those features will influence who we are now and who we will become.

> ...the core principle of ecological psychology – that a person and his or her environment aren't separate entities but form an interdependent behavior setting... a dynamic that influences how we feel and what we do.
> Roger Barker, <u>Ecological Psychology</u>

We all know that 'dressing for the job you want – not the job you have' can help trigger success (that Law of Attraction again). Similarly, when you live in an environment that mirrors the life you <u>want</u> (not the life you <u>have</u>) then your life begins to move in that new direction. It's much harder to get motivated to find a job if you're still living in your high school bedroom with light blue carpet surrounded by My Little Pony figures and posters of Destiny's Child (or black shag carpet and walls with posters of Eminem).

That's exactly why the more generous employers provide laid-off employees with out-placement center services. Calling potential employers from an office in the city is more motivating than calling them from your dining room table with a view of the kitchen sink.

> *The idea that where you are influences who you are and what you'll do sounds so simple that you have to go over it several times before its import really sinks in.*
> *Winifred Gallagher, <u>House Thinking</u>*

Lobby Story: Designing for the Young

One client of mine was the building manager of an historic 1920s office building in San Francisco. The Main Lobby was beautifully detailed with intricate multi-colored marble flooring and a gold-coffered ceiling with period chairs sitting on a plush vintage area rug.

Roseann called me because several technology firms from Shanghai were coming to tour the building as prospective tenants. She wanted some Feng Shui advice and knew that was one of my specialties.

First I described the concept of Mirroring and asked her, *"Does this 1920s Lobby look like someplace a young entrepreneur from China will feel he (or she) belongs?*
That will promote their firm's "coming to California" innovative image?
Attract creative 20-something employees from Shanghai and the Silicon Valley? Give their clients the impression they are a modern, dynamic and expanding international firm?"

Roseann admitted: *"Not really..."*

Her impressively designed building lobby mirrored conservative professionals like attorneys, accountants and financial advisors whose staff and clients would appreciate and feel supported by a classic San Francisco building that looked solid, traditional and established (like their own firms). People prefer places that reinforce and reflect their personal dreams and goals. These places make them feel good about themselves, whether they are consciously aware of this or not. When someone is out-of-sync with an environment, they generally can't describe why. They just know that it isn't a place where they "belong."

> *A person's satisfaction with his or her physical work environment is positively associated with job satisfaction, which is positively correlated with life expectancy and employee well-being and negatively associated with stress, anxiety, depression and low self-esteem.*
> Dak Kopec, <u>Environmental Psychology for Design</u>

So I suggested that my client replace the dark vintage area rug with a high-impact ultra-modern carpet with a bold graphic pattern. And replace the dark Victorian seating group with modern bright white leather lounge chairs and a metal coffee table. These additions would provide a strong contrast with the 1920s architecture. The new carpet and furniture might begin to bridge the gap between the past and future while creating the Impression during the Shanghai tour that young forward-thinking firms could thrive here.

> *Man's character is the product of his premises.*
> *Ayn Rand, The Fountainhead*

> *What you see you become.*
> *Vedic proverb*

Senior Living Story: Designing for the not so Young

If you are designing a senior living facility, think seriously about the environment that will make the elderly occupants feel strong and confident. Later you can consider your own personal design preferences. Their molecules will interact with their environment, so make it someplace that will remind them of their strong and healthy former lives while making them feel comfortable, capable and productive now.

> *Ecology is, by definition, the reciprocal relationship among all organisms and their biological and physical environment.*
> *Frederick Steiner, Human Ecology*

One highly publicized senior living complex was designed a few years ago with a Disneyland Main Street theme in the public areas: 1x1 white and black hexagonal floor tiles in the Barber Shop, colorful linoleum in the Ice Cream Parlor, and traditional tile patterns in the other shops and dining rooms reminiscent of the past. Designing to reinforce a familiar theme may not be typical in a housing complex, but this design scheme was very successful with the residents.

> *Those over age 65 are the fastest growing segment of the population in the industrialized world, and those over age 85 are the fastest growing subgroup of the elderly. In the United States... that number will rise to 20% by 2030. In Japan... 23% by 2020.*
> *Bell, Greene, Fisher and Baum, Environmental Psychology*

Designing to impress and intimidate:
"You are approaching the Wizard of Oz"

My friend Mary, an architect and interior designer in Manhattan, consciously "puts words first" when she designs spaces for her own clients (primarily large corporations). She reminded me that creating "warm and fuzzy" stress-reducing places isn't the goal of every client. Sometimes the best design for a client of Mary's is one that will slightly intimidate lobby visitors. She came up with the following examples of verbal descriptions she develops before putting pencil to paper or mouse to pad (and before selecting specific flooring materials):

- How should the lobby of the American Heart Association look?
  (Grand, corporate and with a noble mandate)
- The lobby of a Telecom Company's Customer Service Center?
  (Informal, personal and caring)
- The lobby of that Telecom Company's Corporate Headquarters?
  (Efficient, capable and corporate. While negotiating labor contracts or disaster recovery plans, the First Impression should be one of power and ethical values - but not informal, personal, caring or a "push-over for the unions").
- The Ground Floor Lobby of a 40-Story High-Rise with multiple International Corporate Headquarters?
  (International, impressive, powerful and larger-than-life)
  Carrying that thinking further, a Roman Plaza pattern mixing granites and marbles could be an appropriate expression.

> Because its impact is primarily subconscious, flooring can also be used to enhance specific qualities within institutional or commercial programs. An organization in need of gravitas, for example, can benefit from heavy marble or plank flooring. One requiring a softer image can help promote a shift in customer appreciation through the introduction of lighter woods, natural carpet or fibers. A need for a more contemporary appeal can be easily promoted with newer applications of older materials, recycled wood, and trendy textures and colors.
> Alex Stark, Feng Shui Consultant

Translating adjectives into specific design recommendations and appropriate material specifications to meet a client's spoken (and often unspoken) goals is the responsibility of designers like Mary.

Later chapters will provide more information describing that process. When you believe (like I do) that people's energetic exchange of molecules with their environment can help or hurt their lives, then your design choices become much more important. <u>You</u> become much more important.

> *An interior environment should reflect who you are, and where you are going. It should capture your vision, support your mission, and help you accomplish your goals.*
> Rosalyn Cama, Ph.D, FASID, EDAC

> *DNA does not control biology, and the nucleus itself is not the brain of the cell. Just like you and me, cells are shaped by where they live. In other words, it's the environment, stupid.*
> Bruce H. Lipton, Ph.D., <u>The Biology of Belief</u>

V. Clients Value a <u>Design with a Purpose</u> Approach

My own clients enjoy hearing me explain how the First Impression of a specific design recommendation could help them in quantifiable ways.

> *For those who wonder where the next project will come from, the competitive advantage offered by tying design to positive client outcomes may be the reason to adopt this model.*
> D. Kirk Hamilton and David H. Watkins,
> <u>Evidence Based Design for Multiple Business Types</u>

Accounting Firm wants a New Carpet to promote a New Goal

When my client, Shea Labagh Dobberstein, a successful San Francisco Accounting firm, renewed their lease after 7 years, the partners asked me to recommend new paint colors and a new carpet to replace their worn cobalt-blue, grey and black small-patterned broadloom carpet.

During my design presentation, I showed them two different design schemes that would work well with their existing interior finishes. I also explained that each would affect their staff differently. The partners were surprised that I spent as much time talking about design psychology as aesthetics when I showed them paint color and carpet alternates.

Alternate #1: The green, cream and black carpet tile alternate with a small geometric pattern would create a new look while maintaining a similar energy level to their existing carpet since both carpets included cool colors and small regular (but different) patterns.

Alternate #2: The gold, tan and terracotta carpet tile alternate with a large organic pattern would increase the energy throughout their office since Alternate #2 had much warmer colors and a larger pattern than the existing carpet. The staff would definitely feel the difference.
(Hidden Messages 3, 5 and 8 describe many of the strategies that will help increase and decrease energy levels through specific floor patterns).

We discussed their business goals and whether their staff would benefit most from a more relaxed atmosphere or a more energized atmosphere. Jim and Greg decided that stress was less of an issue than motivation (except for the very busiest tax month) so they selected the design scheme with the higher energy level to give their staff a psychological lift – with the large-patterned gold, tan and terracotta carpet tile. Like my other clients, they were confident they had made the right choice because there was <u>purpose and intention</u> behind their design decision. Why would they second-guess themselves – or me?

Designing to Meet Client Goals creates a Faster, Easier and More Lasting Client Approval Process

This Design with a Purpose/Architectural Design Psychology Approach makes design presentations much smoother and approvals much easier to obtain. I don't need to try to explain "good design" (an impossible task) or try to convince a client to pay for an upgrade based upon my own subjective design opinion.

My clients are much more willing to approve additional costs that can be justified through increased productivity and comfort (corporations), patient and staff stress-reduction and satisfaction (healthcare), increased tenant leasing (landlords), better behaved and performing students (schools), or happier family members (residential).

> *Flooring sets the stage for all healthcare activities. It contributes to a first impression as people enter and move about a healthcare facility, shaping their opinions about the organization's ability to provide safe, quality and comfortable care.*
> *"Achieving EBD Goals through Flooring Selection & Design",*
> *The Center for Health Design, www.healthdesign.org/chd/research*

> *Office workers who were satisfied with aspects of their environment were more likely to be satisfied with their jobs, indicating a significant relationship between environmental satisfaction and job satisfaction, consistent with previous findings.*
> *(Carlopio, 1996; Ferguson and Weisman, 1986; Sundstrom, 1994; Zalesny, 1985)*

> *With salaries and benefits at $318.00 per square foot (Environmental Building News, April 2005) a one percent increase in productivity equals $3.18 per square foot; a five percent increase in productivity equals $15.90 per square foot... in a 44,000 square-foot building, that five percent productivity increase equals $699,600 per year.*
> *Jenifer Seal Cramer and William Dee Browning in* <u>Biophilic Design</u>

The remaining chapters will help you learn very specific strategies that you can discuss with your own clients and use during the design process.

> *When we investigate the invisible mechanics of nature, we find that everything in the universe is directly connected with everything else. Everything is constantly being influenced by everything else. No wave of the ocean is independent of any other.*
>   Maharishi Mahesh Yogi

> *"Everything communicates. Like it or not."*
>   Bruce Mau, <u>Massive Changes</u>

THIS FIRST IMPRESSION HIDDEN MESSAGE DESCRIBED THE IMPORTANCE OF YOUR VERBALIZING THE DESIGN INTENTIONS THAT ALIGN MOST WITH YOUR CLIENT'S PURPOSE <u>PRIOR</u> TO DEVELOPING DESIGN SKETCHES AND IMAGES.

IT ALSO DESCRIBED HOW YOUR DESIGN CHOICES:
- **CAN TELL OTHERS ABOUT YOUR CLIENT.**
- **WILL INFLUENCE PEOPLE'S PERCEPTION OF THEMSELVES.**
- **CAN CHANGE END-USER BEHAVIOR.**

> *Flooring has a significant impact on aspects of life and business that are seemingly unrelated to its material or technical qualities. The right flooring, for example, can serve as a metaphorical or symbolic trigger for a sense of elegance, a feeling of rustic simplicity, or of casual relaxation.*
>   *On a more subtle plane, this can have a significant impact on the reputation of a business or institution, on the level or satisfaction experienced by staff and visitors, and on the potential for prosperity and success such spaces can promote.*
>   Alex Stark, Feng Shui Consultant

> *Make the places you design the best places for people to live the lives they want to lead. The physical environment alone cannot make everyone's dreams come true, but it sure can tip the scales in one direction or the other.*
> Sally Augustin, PhD,
> *Place Advantage: Applied Psychology for Interior Architecture*

HIDDEN MESSAGE #2:

"Light is Up" and "Grounding is Good"

IN THIS CHAPTER YOU WILL LEARN:
- HOW MONOCHROMATIC FLOOR, WALL AND CEILING COLORS CAN INCREASE ANXIETY.
- HOW GROUNDING THE FLOOR COLOR WILL REDUCE STRESS.

I. The Most Basic Relationship in Nature

"Light is Up" wherever you are

During my college summers, I taught swimming lessons to the 4-year-old Guppy first-timers and I never once needed to tell a hesitant Guppy:

"If you find yourself twisting under the water, swim towards the light – not towards the darkness!"

Not one little Guppy needed THAT information! Swimming "up" for light and air is an instinctive response for every person or animal tossed into the water at any age.

> *In nature, we experience light, medium and dark color values in the light value of the high sky, the midrange values in the objects at our eye level (buildings, forests, distant hills), and the dark value of the earth below our feet...as a result, we tend to feel more comfortable and balanced when the color values we use on our floors, walls and ceilings reflect this natural daytime separation.*
> Vincent Smith, <u>Feng Shui: A Practical Guide for Architects and Designers</u>

As painters and photographers know, when you stand anywhere on earth during the day, the sky is the source of the brightest light (even on a cloudy day). Unlike us, our ancestors spent most of their waking lives outside under bright open skies. They slept indoors during the dark hours to avoid scary predators with better eyesight and bigger teeth.

> *...humans are a largely diurnal animals, heavily reliant on sight for securing resources and avoiding hazard and danger.*
> Stephen Kellert, <u>Biophilic Design</u>

Over hundreds of thousands of years, this relationship in nature, experienced by every creature on earth, developed into one of our human instincts.

It's only been a blip in the course of human history that people have been active after dark (thanks to Thomas Edison). Why should it be surprising that people from every culture, like my Guppies, instinctively know that Light-is-Up and feel most comfortable when building interiors reinforce this relationship?

Does that mean that specifying flooring darker than walls would be a good default position for the majority of your designs? Yes!
Since that is the instinct-based relationship that makes people feel most comfortable, it is common sense that we should have a reason (beyond "good design") for proposing a different relationship.
(See Figure 2.1)

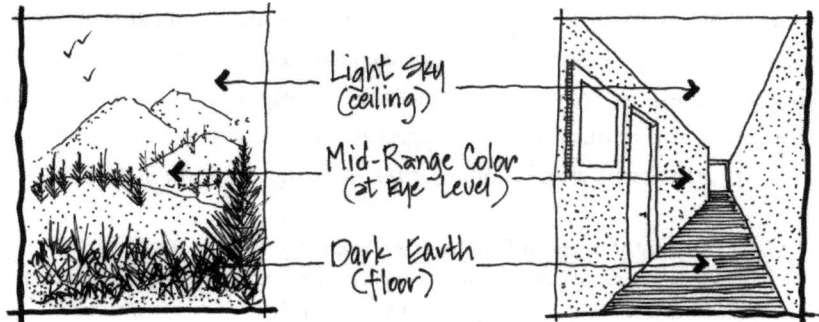

Figure 2.1: *"Light is Up" = the Most Basic Relationship in Nature*

Real Estate Agents Know Best

When you watch *Househunters, Sell This House, Flip This House, Buy This House, Secrets That Sell* or any other home improvement television program, you hear Real Estate Agents advise sellers that *"people want hardwood floors, neutral wall colors and white ceilings."* That's what the typical homebuyers want – and those recommendations follow our unconscious preference for Light-is-Up.

> *The Greek philosopher Heraclitus believed that all things tend to move upward from the moist and dark to the dry light of fire. Sacred architecture urges us to travel through this spectrum of light and shadow...beneath the dome of San Carlo alle Quattro Fontane in Rome, for instance, we are shrouded in murky shadows; our sight is drawn upward to the lantern at the dome's apex, where a dazzling glow calls our spirits to rise heavenward.*
> Anthony Lawlor, <u>The Temple of the House</u>

Even Astronauts Need Grounding

The NASA space stations were initially designed with all of the interior surfaces painted the same light grey color. (Without gravity people just float around so there is no "up"). But after the first space mission, the young and extremely healthy astronauts complained about not feeling comfortable in an all-grey environment. They wanted one surface identified as the ground. So now one surface is always painted a darker color than the others to provide the same relationship astronauts experience on earth in the natural world. Interesting that instincts humans developed on earth are now influencing interior design in outer space!

> *The experience of living on Earth makes humans expect that darker colors will be on lower surfaces and lighter colors on higher ones. Professor Maria Joao Durao from Lisbon Technical University, a participant at the 2007 Senses, Brain and Spaces Workshop, stated that she applied this principle while working on the design of spacecraft interiors in conjunction with the American Institute of Aeronautics.*
> *Use of darker colors lower and lighter colors higher allows space travelers to maintain a sense of balance and avoid unpleasant conditions, such as feeling nauseous.*
> Peter Barrett & Lucinda Barrett, Senses, Brain and Spaces Workshop, 2007

Senior (and weak) Eyes Benefit with Contrasting Walls and Floors

> *75-yr olds see only ½ the contrast that 30-yr-olds do, while 90-yr-olds only see 1/6 the contrast.*
> Journal of Vision Impairments and Blindness, 2000

Read THAT quotation again and then think about who makes the color decisions in your firm. Because he or she sees color contrasts accurately, your 30-year-old designer may think that an a somewhat monochromatic color and finishes scheme will look fine in a senior housing project, while the 85-yr-old residents may feel unstable and unsettled.

> *Even nonslip flooring can be hazardous to patients if it has...a monochromatic color scheme...the use of monochromatic colors in areas that change elevation (e.g., stairs and landings, sunken rooms) can be problematic for those whose brains may be unable to recognize or interpret elevation changes...*
> Dak Kopec, Environmental Psychology for Design

> *(In Subacute Care and Rehabilitation Facilities)* A monochromatic color scheme may be perceived as institutional. It can become monotonous and boring when viewed for an extended period. It can contribute to sensory deprivation when leads to disorganization of brain function, deterioration of intelligence and an inability to concentrate.
>
> Cynthia Leibrock and Debra Harris,
> <u>Design Details for Health: Making the Most of Design's Healing Potential</u>

II. But Designers <u>Love</u> Monochromatic Bubbles…

They're Everywhere! They're Everywhere!

A few years ago I collected magazine photos to illustrate this principle for a seminar I gave at a national AIA Conference. I was amazed to find that while 80% of the photographs in non-professional design magazines (*House & Garden, Architectural Digest* etc.) had darker flooring than walls, the opposite was true in my professional magazines (*Interior Design, Architectural Record, Architect*).

Approximately 80% of the photographs in professional magazines showcased award-winning projects following a color concept I call,

"The Monochromatic Bubble":

- Bedrooms with beige carpet, walls, beige upholstery and linens.
- Restaurants with concrete floors, concrete walls and stairs.
- Law Offices with grey tile and carpeting, grey glossy wall panels, metal and grey lounge seating and grey workstations.

All Monochromatic Bubbles! Once I realized this, I saw bubbles everywhere. It seems that designers around the planet love the challenge of designing projects that are all white, all beige or all grey (with the occasional all red or all yellow schemes for the most adventurous).

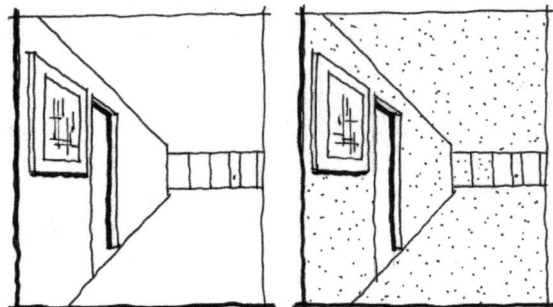

Figure 2.2 and 2.3: *Monochromatic Bubbles*

And I believe that I REALLY annoyed my architect-husband, 2007 National President of the AIA, during the dozens of design award ceremonies we attended. I kept whispering "monochromatic bubble" every time someone won an Interior Design award and a photograph flashed overhead in cities including Washington D.C., San Francisco, Los Angeles, New York, London and Melbourne. Monochromatic Bubbles are obviously an international design favorite.

A White Project for the Wrong Client

My friend, Shelley, was Alumna Director for a major university in Texas a few years ago when her school was planning a new Alumna Center. She attended one of my Seminars where I described the popularity of Monochromatic Bubbles. Afterwards she told me,

"NOW I understand! We've had two design presentations and both times the designers asked us to approve white carpet and white porcelain tile. They kept saying how easy it is now to clean high quality white wool carpet.

Our Committee told the designers that one of the main purposes of the building is giving parties after football games. Alumna will be served beer, wine and other drinks that could end up on the floor. But the designers keep pushing white floors and we couldn't understand why!"

I explained that the senior project designer had probably not yet designed his/her White Project and Shelley needed to be firm about their need for darker alcohol-masking flooring. The designer could create a White Project for a more appropriate client in the future.

Final Chapter: Shelley went back and talked to her committee members and the designers. Now their alumna can spill beer and wine on darker carpets and tile (feeling very comfortable and grounded at the same time) while they write those big checks.

Of course to be honest, while I never designed a White Project, I did design a Beige Project for a law firm in San Jose in the 1990s – blending creams, beiges and tans in carpet, marble tiles, walls, leather furniture, counters, glossy doors and millwork. I thought it looked extremely elegant and understated. Our art-collecting client agreed.

During the photo shoot, I remember adjusting the Conference Room louver drapes to create a pattern on the tan broadloom carpet, and placing a vase of red gladiolas at the end of the corridor. Now I see that photo and I think, "Of course it needed a louver drape pattern and red flowers! Without those, it looked way too monotonous – monotonously elegant, but still monotonous."

> It appears that exposing the subject to a monotonous sensory environment can cause disorganization of brain function similar to, and in some respects as great as, that produced by drugs or lesions...
> Blank surfaces tend to fade out if viewed continuously. Even colors may fade into neutral gray. Vision seems to degenerate unless simulated, and the mind itself drops into lethargy.
>   Faber Birren, Color & Human Response

In retrospect I believe it was lucky that those attorneys were all young and working with equally young tech-company clients. They didn't suffer by working in a beige bubble.

Re-Creating Nature's Most Dangerous Color Relationships

Question: What conditions in the natural world produce monochromatic bubbles?
Answer: <u>Dangerous</u> weather conditions!

Our ancestors' Light-is-Up instinct also kept them safe in the most dangerous weather when their survival depended upon retreating into caves and communal huts to wait out white snowstorms, tan sandstorms, thick grey fog and black starless nights (all monochromatic bubbles).

> *When upholstery, walls, ceilings, and other elements in the room are all fundamentally white or beige, we get tense.*
> *(Mahnke, 1996)*

Think about all those episodes in old westerns and programs like *Little House on the Prairie* and *Love Comes Softly* where someone was lost in a blinding snowstorm somewhere between the barn and the house. Only banging pots and rifle shots brought them safely back to the kitchen door (their beards or hair covered with icicles). Our instincts rebel against similar monochromatic interior environments because we subconsciously equate them with dangerous natural environments. Projects that are predominantly white seem to cause particular problems.

> *A recent study demonstrated that... elderly people's attentional impairments are worsened in low light, low contrast, and glare conditions... Designers should be aware of glare issues, especially those created from using white on white.*
> Dak Kopec, <u>Environmental Psychology for Design</u>

> *All white environments not only create glare but also under-stimulate the eyes. Under-stimulation can result in eye fatigue just as overstimulation can.*
> Baughan-Young, Kim. "What Color is Success?", 2002
> *TFM (Today's Facility Manager)*

Why do Designers Love Monochromatic Bubbles?

So... scientific studies, home improvement television programs, design magazines for non-professionals, and NASA astronauts support the Light-is-Up principle – while designers and architects shower awards on Monochromatic Bubble Designs. *What's up with THAT???*

This contradiction stems from the fact that our education and experience train us to "see" space differently. My professors in graduate school tried to inspire me to "push the envelope" to create unique and interesting buildings as an architectural student the same way I was inspired to create unique and interesting art projects as an undergraduate art student. It seemed logical for me to conceive of architecture as sculpture.

> *Along with the basic knowledge we acquire, we seem to learn a 'way of seeing' that is characteristic of our chosen profession...*
> Robert Gifford, Environmental Psychology Principles and Practice

The Monochromatic Bubble feels edgier, slightly unsettling and "different" – all feelings creative people have been taught to appreciate. Designers don't want to feel that their work is boring and repetitive. Isn't "turning the mundane into the sublime" a goal in every creative field from dancing and writing to design?

Most of us grew up in homes with darker flooring, medium or neutral wall colors, and light ceilings. Why would designers think <u>that</u> scheme would be an interesting aesthetic choice?

Thompson Penney, 2003 National AIA President, described the typical architect's perspective at an Academy of Neuroscience for Architecture (ANFA) Conference that explored the relationship between the brain and design.

Thom said, *"Architects worship the gods of novelty and originality."*

The pursuit of novelty and originality (including the challenge of successfully blending dozens of monochromatic colors and materials like greys, whites and metallic finishes) may make daytime design careers more stimulating and enjoyable, but it doesn't have anything to do with comfort and health. Our need for more stimuli hasn't changed in hundreds of thousands of years according to scientists.

> *... monotony may lead the animal to starve itself, to overeat, to refuse to procreate, and to devour and destroy its kind or any other kind. Apes have been observed to withdraw within themselves in the manner of schizophrenics if left alone or surrounded by blank walls.*
> Faber Birren, Color & Human Response

Okay, that quote is a little severe (although definitely in keeping with life-and-death caveman thinking). The following section describes places where monochromatic design schemes do promote the personal and professional goals of the client and end-users.

III. Positive Places for Monochromatic Bubbles

The Dark Sky Restaurant Exception

Many restaurants violate the Light-is-Up relationship in nature with very dark ceiling finishes and colors. Sometimes these dark ceilings hide unsightly mechanical ducts and ceiling construction, and other times this scheme is used to reinforce the cozy atmosphere of clustering around candlelight or eating under the stars. (See Figure 2.4)

Evolutionary Psychologists and Neuroscientists say that we all have a strong instinctive attraction to fire and hearth, regardless of age, culture or health. (This takes us back to "caveman thinking" when our ancestors must have felt great relief returning after a hard day of hunting to the safety in numbers of their clan gathered around a campfire in the darkness.)

> *It is hypothesized that there are universal pre-set, and hardwired memories common to all humans that can be used in design to achieve certain goals...*
>
> *... hearth, fire, food, sunlight and weather... generate brain responses in people of all age groups from school children to the elderly. Such responses are suggested to reduce stress response and produce a calming effect by generating a greater sense of "feeling at home".*
> The Academy of Neuroscience for Architecture Conference, Woodshole 2004

The Retail Bubble Exception

The next time you go into a very high-end department store like Neiman Marcus, look for the designer boutiques clustered along the perimeter. Many are successfully designed with monochromatic colors that reinforce their brand. In some cases the flooring material (carpet, laminate or tile) wraps seamlessly from the floor up onto the walls.

When the architectural envelope is monochromatic (floors, walls and ceilings, or floors and walls minimally) then the objects inside REALLY call attention to themselves, like twenty brightly colored $500 leather purses against an all-white background, or all-black designer clothes showcased in an all-yellow store environment. (See Figure 2.5)

Figure 2.4   **Figure 2.5:**
Restaurant and Retail Monochromatic Bubble Exceptions

The Very Dark Climate Exception

I described this principle to a friend who had just returned from a trip to Scandinavia. She remarked that most of the residential interiors she saw were painted white (including hardwood floors with pale-colored accent rugs) to counteract the long days of darkness.

Since science has confirmed our biological and psychological need for light (problems with Vitamin D deficiency and SADS, for example) it seems that physical needs can trump our real (but less critical) preference for feeling grounded.

The Very Creative Client Exception

Sometimes I see a space with a monochromatic color scheme and I experience bliss - like walking alone through the white-arched promenade in Santiago Calatrava's Milwaukee Art Museum after-hours while attending an AIA party in another wing (a real plus to joining the AIA or IIDA; events are held in fabulous places).

I felt like I was stepping through the clouds – the definition of "sublime". His monochromatic museums, bridges and transportation projects can lift architecture to inspirational realms, like Gothic Cathedrals have done for centuries. Calatrava (a Spanish architect, structural engineer, sculptor and painter) creates contrast in his all-white structures by manipulating light across unique structural forms and elements.

These are also places that people walk through, not places where people live or where many work.

Monochromatic Bubbles can also be appropriate for some very high-budget corporate and residential clients whose aesthetic preferences match those of their designers.

For years I saw exquisite bubble projects featured in Interior Design, Architect and Architectural Record Magazines that were designed by my friend from SOM-days, interior architect Lauren Rottet.

I used to think,

"Lauren's beautiful monochromatic 'white finishes and white furniture everywhere' projects <u>must</u> be unhealthy for end-users!"

But then I read the research confirming that people can be trained to "see" space differently. And I realized that Lauren's clients (unlike mine and most designers') are corporate and professional moguls with the ability to lease much more space than they actually need, typically share their designer's aesthetic taste before the project even begins, and have very large construction and furniture budgets.

Their spaces usually feature very few people populating gigantic open interior spaces showcasing classic and custom furniture with fabulous and phenomenally expensive art collections. Most of her clients have been trained by their backgrounds and experience to "see" space the same way Lauren does long before they become her clients.

Lauren stresses the importance of a designer's "<u>completely</u> finishing and furnishing" an architectural space with great attention to detail. On her own projects, she specifies rich decorative finishes, textures and materials; both artificial and natural lighting sources; a variety of hard and soft flooring types; with high quality furniture, artwork and accessories. Using these elements she identifies "pausing places" that attract the viewers' eyes from one place to another as they move through the space.

The success of this design approach depends greatly upon budget as well as expertise, since value engineering can quickly eliminate the textural richness required to elevate a project from a deadening and unhealthy monochromatic bubble to an elegant and healthy place for people.

"Know Thy Client"

You can probably think of other project types and situations where a monochromatic design scheme can promote client goals. But designers shouldn't try to turn low or medium-budget projects into these exceptions by arm-twisting more typical clients and thinking,

"If only my clients could see the final design, then they would love it!"

Research has proven that won't happen unless your client leaves his day job and attends design school!

When you consciously try to Design with a Purpose, *"Know your client"* is just as good advice as *"know yourself."*

Grounding Flooring Design Action Steps:

1. Think about the goals and health of your clients and end-users before developing color scheme alternates. Unless you have a reason to violate the Light-is-Up relationship, the best strategy is defaulting to a grounding color scheme.

2. Healthcare, senior-living facilities and interiors for the vision-impaired should include darker floors that clearly contrast with the walls to promote comfort and confidence.

3. While individual clients with design knowledge might experience the edginess of a monochromatic design scheme positively, if a group of people will share the space, it is wiser to "design for the greatest good" and ground the design.

4. If you are selecting flooring for young and healthy people who will not be staying inside a space for a long period of time (not workplaces or schools) then grounding is not as important.

5. This principle can also be applied to the design of elevator cabs where inflicting a "grey-patterned-floor-with-polished-metal geometric-wall-panels-and-glaring-bright-light" design scheme on unsuspecting patients going into a rehab clinic from the parking garage seemed cruel (a real example).
They might love that design aesthetic at Facebook.
(But the surprised older guy on crutches? Not so much.)

6. If you are asked to furnish an interior that has existing monochromatic finishes, you can ground the space with darker area rugs. To turn walls in a monochromatic scheme into a mid-range color, adding artwork can be a fast and effective solution.

7. Always put flooring samples on the floor and then step back to view the overall scheme the way end-users will.

8. When in doubt about tonal relationships, apply the Squint Test to determine the overall floor and wall contrast.

IN THIS CHAPTER YOU LEARNED THAT YOUR DEFAULT DESIGN CHOICE SHOULD REINFORCE THE LIGHT-IS-UP RELATIONSHIP IN NATURE IN ORDER TO REDUCE STRESS AND INCREASE COMFORT.

If you are Designing with a Purpose (in a verbalized and agreed-upon client-specific situation) then go for the Bubble!

Otherwise – stay grounded. Like Conan and the Astronauts.

> *The brain requires continuous new information, in the form of change and stimulation, to maintain homeostasis or balance between internal and external environments.... A combination of white walls, white ceiling, and other white elements in the space can upset patients.*
> Jane Rohde, *"Exploring the Evidence,"* 2007 Healthcare Design Conference

HIDDEN MESSAGE #3:

A Line on the Ground = A Change in Plane

IN THIS CHAPTER YOU WILL LEARN WHEN HIGH CONTRAST COLORS AND PATTERNS CAN CREATE UNSAFE WALKING CONDITIONS.

> *The larger the scale of the design, the smaller the group of people the pattern appeals to... There may be evolutionary biological explanations, or lifestyle / behavioral factors at work. A fatigued individual probably is less likely to select a "busy" combination of florals. Perhaps in our distant past, busy florals in a setting of heavy vegetation concealed danger.*
> (Rodemann, 1999)

In nature, every time there is a different color on the ground it typically means that the height of the ground changes at the "line" between the two surfaces. Think about your own experiences at a park, playground or beach. Sand to dirt, grass to stone, forest path to field; every "line" on the ground means you either need to step up or step down.

Figures 3.1 and 3.2: *A Line on the Ground = A Change in Plane*

If you just shuffle your feet across the pavement onto a clump of grass without looking down and lifting your foot, then you will probably fall flat on your face. Since looking down has always been (and still is) a necessary survival strategy, flooring design may be the most important feature in the environments we create for ourselves and for others.

> *Through evolution we have tuned our attentional system to be more sensitive to objects in our lower visual field... (since our ancestors were more likely to find tracks of prey and lurking predators on the ground and in bushes than up in the trees). This enhanced capacity to process information in our lower field is consistent with there being more connections to the parietal lobe from the part of the visual brain that represents the lower field.*
> (Gazzaniga, 1998)

I. Instinctive Reactions to Lines on the Ground

Tentative Toddler Walking Story

I described this principle when I taught a half-day Architectural Design Psychology seminar to the staff of a west coast architectural firm. The Senior Project Designer, David, said,

"That describes my son! Josh is 14 months old, starting to walk on his own, and doesn't want me to hold onto his hand anymore. But every time he reaches a joint in a sidewalk, his arm pops up and he won't move until I hold his hand again. He isn't sure if he can walk over the joint on his own. And it's just a line in the concrete."

Amazing, because there are probably just a few weeks in a child's life when he consciously recognizes something the rest of us have long forgotten. A month from now when Josh's comprehension and coordination improves his little body will unconsciously make the physical adjustments to easily step over that same line in the ground (or he will understand that the concrete on both sides of the line is the same height so he won't pause). His hand won't shoot up again.

That's human instinct in action! David's son didn't have a clue what a line on the ground meant, but something deep inside told him that he would need help crossing safely.

Dozens of times each day, when we see a line or color change on the ground or floor ahead (especially in unfamiliar places), we unconsciously prepare ourselves to step over it by changing our stride so we can pick up our feet up slightly when we reach it. Our bodies tense when we adjust our steps. This creates a little stress that generally doesn't bother us. But this process can create a lot <u>more</u> stress if we are older, sick or are just feeling wobbly for any reason.

> *Be aware of design elements that may increase elderly people's fears of falling, such as angles, distances, and surface textures... Falls are a leading cause of death among the elderly...*
> Dak Kopec, <u>Environmental Psychology for Design</u>

Tentative Grandmother Walking Story

I also shared the concept that "a Line on the Ground equals a Change in Plane" when I gave a one-day Wayfinding Workshop to the design team of a major medical center in Washington D.C. One of the designers jumped in and said,

"That must be what was happening when I took my grandmother to see her doctor last week! We walked into the Lobby of an old medical office building downtown and she kept stopping every few feet. Finally I said, "Grandma, let's go, we'll be late!" and practically dragged her across the lobby.

She must have thought that the elaborate marble floor pattern might include steps. I had no idea why she kept stopping."

> *...even nonslip flooring can be hazardous to patients if it has a strong pattern... Brighter colors against darker backgrounds can create the illusion of three-dimensionality, which can lead to disorientation and falls among patients who suffer from cognitive degeneration; therefore, avoid the use of highly contrasting colors.*
>
> Dak Kopec, <u>Environmental Psychology for Design</u>

Tentative Uncle-in-the-Hospital Walking Story

A few years ago I was asked to review a full-scale mock-up of a hospital patient room by a San Francisco architectural firm specializing in Healthcare. The designers were enthused because a linoleum manufacturer had volunteered to donate the flooring material as well as labor to create a dramatic striped pattern with three colors curving from wall to wall in the room that would travel to a variety of Expo floors.

My "designer brain" was impressed. I thought the linoleum floor pattern made the patient room much more interesting and unusual. And I liked the blend of colors. But then my Ethel from Modesto avatar reminded me about her 82-yr-old Uncle George, recovering from hip replacement surgery. While he was still groggy from the drugs, George would need to step across <u>five wavy lines</u> just to get from his bed to the bathroom. Uncle George would think he's hallucinating! (See Figure 3.3)

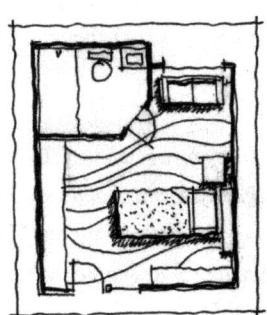

Figure 3.3
Unexpected Lines on the Floor = A Patient Tripping Hazard

What about that floor pattern would seem normal to Uncle George? Nothing! I can't think of any bedroom I've seen in a house or a hotel with stripes extending from wall to wall. Can you? And wavy? Uncle George will tense his body in case one stripe defines a carpet or a different texture (because he doesn't have a clue) and he could easily fall.

That floor pattern would make the journey from bed to bathroom (already considered by hospitals to be a primary area for tripping and falling) much more dangerous than it needed to be. So the Ethel side of me recommended that the designers re-think that dramatic pattern.

> *Hospital patients may undergo surgery that affects their mobility or memory, and they may need sedation, pain relief, anesthetic or other medication, which can increase the risk of falling.*
> *"Slips, Trips and Falls in Hospital", National Patient Safety Agency, PSO/3*

Safe Places for Flooring Transitions

Question: Where can color transition lines happen safely regardless of the project type?

Answer: Wherever elevation changes happen at home (since we take this unconscious knowledge with us into the outside world and react similarly).

In our homes we expect height changes:
- At an area rug below the dining room table or under a bed.
- At an area rug below seating in a Family or Living Room.
- At both sides of a corridor or stairway carpet runner.
- At a doorway threshold between rooms.

Unstable-Feeling Hospital Staff Table Example

One HMO asked me to attend key design presentations where their architects presented Design Alternates for their new Medical Center. At one meeting the team presented Floor Finish Plans that showed large vinyl sheet flooring areas with a variety of colors in internal staff areas. The color combinations and the floor pattern design looked interesting. Then we reviewed the furniture plans and saw that the floor patterns had nothing to do with furniture placement.

A large Staff Table (the size of a conference table) sat partially on a large dark-colored vinyl stripe. Psychologically, people sitting around that table could feel "unsupported", since the dark stripe would subconsciously remind people of an area rug. When my avatar, Ethel, thought about the staff members' frame of reference (dining room tables), she knew that nobody would ever locate a table partway on an area rug. The chairs would constantly fall off a ½" rug thickness causing a constant "thumping" and a falling sensation. Staff would instinctively expect the same plane change as they pushed their chairs away from the Staff Table across a stripe edge – adding a little more stress to already over-worked staff members in need of stress <u>reduction</u>.

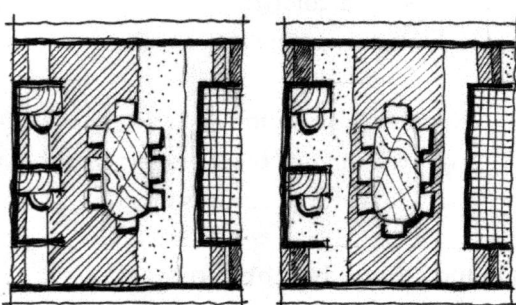

Figure 3.4 and 3.5: *Visually Unsupported and Supported Tables. Which would feel more stable to frazzled nurses?*

It is typical on fast-paced projects that one person designs the floor pattern and another lays out the furniture (often people from two separate

FLOORING PSYCH • 67

departments or firms) and neither has time to think about the other. So no one questioned the appropriateness of an edgy and imbalanced design in a place where anxious hospital staff members go to relax. (That gets back to the need to Program in order to define specific client goals.)

When flooring materials change, designers are very careful to coordinate the different finished floor heights. But changing color alone generally doesn't trigger the same level of coordination. It should! I recommended shifting the stripe pattern slightly so the conference table and surrounding chairs sat entirely on the dark vinyl stripe.
(See Figures 3.4 and 3.5)

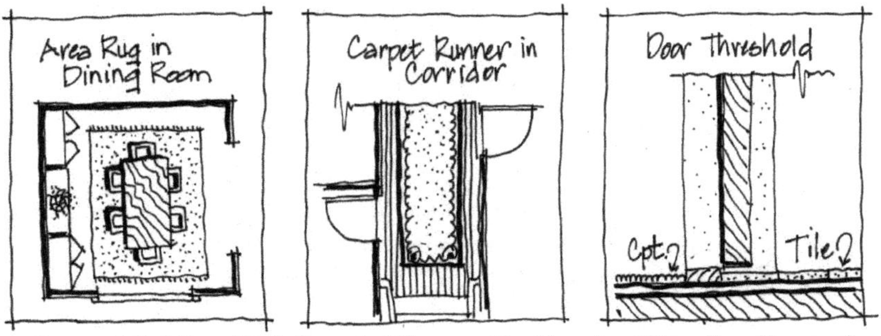

Figures 3.6, 3.7 and 3.8: *Expected Lines on the Floor (and Elevation Changes)*

Figures 3.6, 3.7 and 3.8 show places where people anticipate flooring transitions to occur. They will expect patterns that resemble any of those residential details in other project types. These flooring patterns will feel familiar so people will be able to self-correct unconsciously regardless of their health.

> *Patients suffering from Alzheimer's frequently have impaired depth perception. This causes them to perceive lines on the floor as steps or cliffs. When they alter their gait to negotiate the illusory obstacle, they sometimes fall and sustain life-threatening fractures, especially of the hip. By adjusting the texture of the floor in assisted-living residences, designers can reduce misperceptions and the incidence of falls.*
>
> Dr. Esther Sternberg, <u>Healing Spaces</u>

II.   Are we designing because we <u>can</u> and not because we <u>should</u>?

I am often stunned when I open up magazines like *Healthcare Design, Interior Design, Architect* or *Architectural Record* and see project photographs with amazingly elaborate and colorful accent floor patterns in healthcare and senior housing facilities that don't anticipate the age, eyesight or health condition of the end-users.

Flooring manufacturers should be understandably proud of their recently developed seaming technologies that allow complex patterns in vinyl, rubber, linoleum and carpet. But this opportunity comes with a responsibility. Designers and facility managers need to recognize how much color and complexity might be TOO much color and complexity for specific project types and end-users.

> *It is characteristic of experts to be unaware that their perception of a situation differs from the perception of those who do not share their expertise.*
> Rachel Kaplan, Stephen Kaplan and Robert L. Ryan, <u>With People in Mind</u>

How to Locate Accent Patterns Safely

> *The fact is that when we enter any building, we need a series of steps just to make the adjustments between out there and in here. You need to slow your walk a little, allow your eyes to adjust to the change in lighting, give your senses a chance to detect changes in temperature and so on.*

> *You walk through any door and suddenly your brain has to take in a load of new information and process it so you'll feel oriented... This transition stage is one of the most critical things we've learned in two decades of studying how shoppers move through retail environments.*
> Paco Underhill, <u>Call of the Mall</u>

I described Paco Underhill's transition zone during my *Floor Patterns in Healthcare Facilities: Friend or Foe?* seminar at the Healthcare Design Conference in 2011. A member of a Canadian Hospital's Design Committee came up to me afterwards to tell me about a flooring design that their Interior Designers had just proposed; brightly-colored 10-foot-diameter custom-designed vinyl flooring inlays just a few feet inside the three major entrances.

Laura asked me, *"What do you think about that?"*

I asked Laura,   *"What do YOU think about that after hearing about the 10 to 15 foot transition zone?*

Laura said she could imagine people hurrying into the Hospital Lobbies through the revolving doors to get out of the wind and snow, stopping short at the colorful floor designs, and then piling into each other. She told me she was going back to tell the board that the accent inlays needed to be at least 15 feet inside each lobby. (See Figures 3.13 and 3.14)

She told me,   *"That could have been a disaster!*
               And your recommendation makes such common sense!
               Why didn't we think of that?"

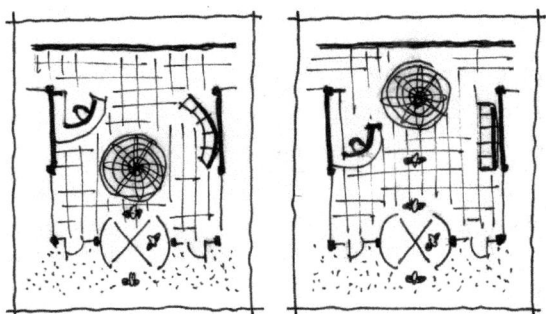

Figure 3.13 and 14:
An Accent Pattern too close to the door and one in a safer location

It is common sense – but only if you have switched your Instinctive-Experiential Brain "on" to understand how a cold, wet and anxious patient night react, and aren't salivating over the ability to use new seaming technology to create dramatic views of old Vancouver that will look fantastic in the *Hospital Journal* and those impressive design magazines.

III. Accent Flooring Design Action Steps:

1. Develop three or four floor pattern alternates, and evaluate them using your Instinctive-Experiential Brain by imagining end-users like:
   - Boisterous 8-yr-old Mars racing into his classroom.
   - 81-yr old Marie speed-walking inside the retail mall.
   - PR VP Lisa on her cell phone rushing through the lobby.
   - Exhausted Emily dragging her screaming toddler thru the Clinic.
   - Organizer Elizabeth carrying a high stack of boxes out of the store.

   Would a particular pattern (lines on the floor) be distracting and make their lives more difficult as they hurry from place to place?

2. That will help you decide if your proposed pattern alternates are appropriate for your project type. If appropriate, would they feel comfortable and promote safety in <u>every</u> room or area within your building - or only in specific places?

3. Next, evaluate the contrast level in your flooring patterns. If you feel your high-contrast multi-colored pattern may cause problems, then you may be able to substitute lower-contrast colors.

(In a mental hospital) optical illusions can be unintentionally created so darker patterns appear raised. Patients may feel they are walking on steps when they approach darker colored tiles after lighter ones. Prominent designs might force compulsive or obsessive patients to zig-zag while walking through a corridor.
"Floor Designs Can Be Therapeutic", Robert Sommmer

FLOORING PSYCH • 71

4. Always coordinate the Furniture Plan with the Floor Finishes Plan before making final design decisions to make sure the flooring "supports" the furniture visually and psychologically.

5. If you have any questions, then think like your Avatar and look for familiar residential references.
Or think like a Caveman and look for references from nature.

6. Try to avoid intellectual rationalization. If you need "design-speak" (that someone outside the design profession would not understand) to justify your pattern choices, then that means you might be designing to please other designers more than the future occupants.

> Sometimes while listening to designers discussing the needs of office workers, students in dormitories, or mental patients, one can learn more about the speaker's own needs than about the needs of his customers.
> One reason for this is the social distance between the architect and the people for whom he is designing.
> Robert Sommer, <u>Personal Space</u>

IN THIS CHAPTER YOU LEARNED THAT PEOPLE MIGHT INSTINCTIVELY INTERPRET A LINE ON THE FLOOR AS A CHANGE OF PLANE.

THAT UNDERSTANDING WILL HELP YOU IDENTIFY WHEN AND WHERE TO LOCATE PATTERNS AND LINES IN ORDER TO MAKE YOUR DESIGNS BOTH SAFE <u>AND</u> AESTHETICALLY PLEASING.

> Patient falls have both human and financial costs. For individual patients, the consequences can range from distress and loss of confidence, to injuries that cause pain and suffering, loss of independence and, occasionally, death.
> "Slips, Trips and Falls in Hospital", National Patient Safety Agency, PSO/3

HIDDEN MESSAGE #4:

Don't Step into the Shadows…

(This concept came from Landscape Designers who seem to be WAY ahead of the rest of us in understanding that Mother Nature knows best)

IN THIS CHAPTER YOU WILL LEARN HOW OUR INSTINCTIVE FEAR OF THE SHADOWS INFLUENCES WHERE WE POSITION OURSELVES AND HOW CONFIDENT WE FEEL WALKING IN CORRIDORS.

A few years ago I attended a seminar at a Senior Living Complex in San Francisco that had just won a design award for its new rooftop garden. The speaker was a Landscape Architect who discussed the special issues involved in designing gardens for the elderly. That was the first time I had ever heard the word "cliffing" and I immediately understood that this idea should be just as important to everyone designing floor patterns <u>inside</u> buildings as it is to landscapers designing paving patterns <u>outside</u> buildings.

What is Cliffing?

The speaker described cliffing as the deep shadows cast by bushes and low walls on otherwise sunny walkways. Identifying potential shadow locations by understanding sun angles is extremely important when landscape designers plan paving and landscaping in healthcare and senior living complexes. She said that even with a four-foot wide flat concrete walkway, for example, if two feet of that width is in the shade, then elderly residents with declining eyesight will wobble single-file in the middle of the remaining two-foot wide sunlit strip in order to avoid the shadows! They can see what's happening in the sunlit area but are worried about what's happening in the shade. (See Figures 4.1 A & B)

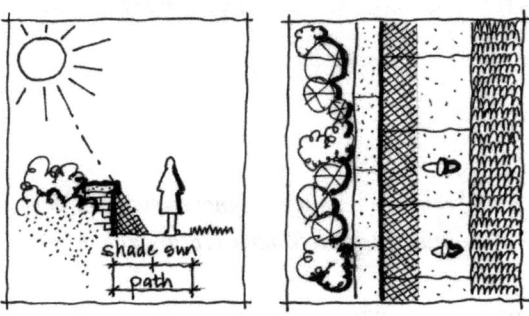

Figure 4.1 A & B
"Walking in the Light" (Cliffing in Section and Plan)

> *"Cliffing" is a term for the perception, often experienced in older adults, of strong contrasting dark shadows on light pavement as changes in grade – steps up or down, which can lead to anxiety and even, in some cases, falls.*
> Naomi Sachs, Therapeutic Landscapes Network,
> *"Exploring the Connection between Nature and Health"*

Remember, studies show that 75-yr-olds see only half the contrast that 30-yr-olds do, while 90-yr-olds see only 1/6 the contrast. So while younger eyes can see that it's safe to walk on shadowed pavement, the elderly or vision-impaired don't know if the shadowed area includes flat paving, a step, fallen branches or a mound of leaves.

> *Dark shadows... on paving can lead to stumbling as aging eyes experience "visual cliffing", darker tones perceived as troughs to be stepped over.*
> Healing Gardens Evaluation, ASLA 2009 Annual Meeting

> *...note the visual phenomena of "cliffing" in older adults: avoid shade structures such as unplanted or unscreened arbors that have strong contrasting light and dark lines on the ground plane creating a striped effect.*
> "Residential Healthcare Facilities", The Center for Health Design, July 2012

Humans have always feared "the shadows". As I described in the Light-is-Up chapter, we developed biologically over hundreds of thousands of years avoiding the darkness where creatures with large fangs and teeth slithered and crept. Every Caveman needing shelter in a storm probably looked for a large open cave where he could see clearly into the corners - not one with deep and mysterious dark shadows "where evil lurks..."

Isn't that what _you_ would do?

Now Add in Centering

When you combine our instinctive preference to stay out of the shadows with our natural tendency to center our bodies within a walkway so we don't bump into things along the sides, then designing with Cliffing and Centering becomes an important strategy for everyone making floor pattern design decisions.

Centering Our Bodies: Outside

Outside, if we walk in the center of any type of pathway, then we are less likely to twist an ankle by stepping off the path, or scrape our legs on prickly plants or shrubs. (See Figure 4.2)

Centering Our Bodies: Inside

We do the same thing inside buildings when we:
- Push our carts down the middle of a supermarket aisle so we don't bump things off the shelves.
- Walk down the center of a hotel corridor so our rolling suitcase doesn't hit the wall. (See Figure 4.3)

Even if there are no shelves, furniture, or plants to avoid, we still feel safer walking in the center of a corridor or aisle.

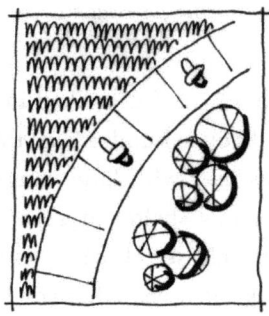 

Figure 4.2:
Centering on a Sidewalk

Figure 4.3
Centering in a Hotel Corridor

A home or an office is not merely an inanimate form or an empty shell where we live and work and through which we walk. Its shape takes on meaning that we recognize and react to, consciously and subconsciously... determining our habits, reactions and effectiveness.
   Sarah Rossbach, <u>Interior Design with Feng Shui</u>

Once I understood the concepts of Cliffing and Centering, then I realized that while we don't generally consider these issues when we design floor patterns in corridors, we should!

So I developed a few <u>Interior</u> Cliffing and Centering Concepts that I apply when I review and compare floor patterns as a consultant:

I.   Cliffing / Centering Concept #1:

<u>People feel safer when corridor floor colors contrast with wall colors. Then the vision-impaired, sick or elderly can easily identify the entire width of the corridor and can safely and confidently position their bodies toward the center.</u>

> *Contrast between the wall and the floor helps to define boundaries.*
> *Cynthia Leibrock and Debra Harris, <u>Design Details for Health</u>*

Centering our bodies in a corridor, a small room and between pieces of furniture feels more comfortable to people for another reason: **<u>It reminds us of home.</u>**

- Many homes have a carpet runner extending down the center of a wood stairway or corridor. We all know that the carpet is higher than the wood floor by at least ¼ of an inch, so we unconsciously place our feet near the center of the runner to avoid stepping off the carpet and tripping.
- At home people might have bookcases, a narrow console, deep picture frames or family clutter along a corridor wall. Walking in the center of the corridor keeps us from bumping into these objects and losing our balance.

We carry our preference for centering our bodies in small home corridors and rooms into the outside world without even thinking about it.

Cliffing and Centering Examples:

> But first: THE SQUINT TEST!
> Important note for the following examples and others throughout this book: when I say "dark grey flooring", it doesn't mean that I'm recommending grey (definitely not). I'm also not referring exclusively to solid-colored materials.
>
> Most carpet, vinyl, linoleum, stone and tile pieces contain multiple colors and flecks. When I say "dark grey" or "light grey" it means that if you step back and squint your eyes, than the overall floor or wall color looks dark grey or light grey. That is what's important – <u>the overall impression and the contrast when you squint</u>. Not the color.

- **Dark Grey Floor + Cream Walls**

A high contrast between the floor and walls makes it easy to identify the width of the walkable corridor. (See Figure 4.4)

- **Medium Grey Floor + Light Grey Walls**

Squint. Do the floor and wall colors blend into each other? If so, then occupants could have a problem figuring out where the floor ends and the wall starts. The vision-impaired might have trouble safely positioning their bodies in the center. This is a concern even if the wall tones aren't the same color, but are close in value or color – like a blue-grey linoleum floor with green painted walls. (See Figure 4.5)

- **Medium Grey Floor + Light Grey Walls + Black Base**

No problem here. People will automatically know that the wall starts at the black base. Providing a contrasting (much darker or much lighter) base is a good way to identify transitions between floors and walls if the colors of the horizontal and vertical surfaces blend together when you squint. (See Figure 4.6)

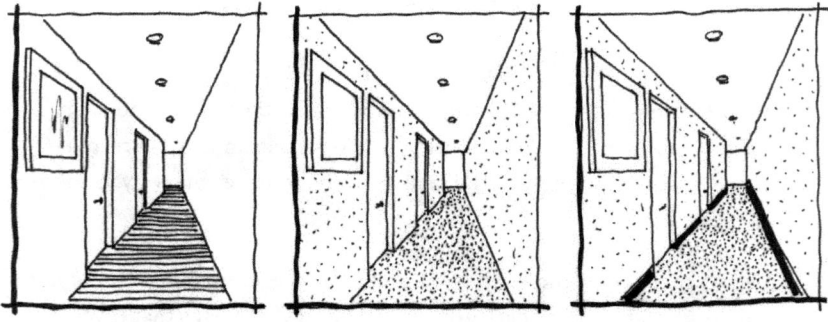

Figure 4.4   **Figure 4.5**   **Figure 4.6:**
Use the Squint Test to see how easy it would be for someone with impaired vision to center his or her body in each of these three corridors with typical floor and wall contrast relationships

II. Cliffing / Centering Concept #2:

<u>Floor colors should contrast with furniture, cabinetry, columns, planters and everything else that springs from or sits on the floor in order to help your end-user avoid bumping into things and tripping.</u>

It was ironic that immediately following the seminar on Healing Gardens where I first heard about cliffing (and thought that Landscape Designers were SO far ahead of the rest of us in thinking about how design affects behavior), we took a tour of the award-winning roof garden.

The Landscape Architect talked about the psychological benefits of assigning planting beds to individual tenants so they could "work the earth" to grow vegetables and flowers. She also discussed the advantages of raised planters (about 17 inches high) so elderly tenants did not need to bend over to garden. But I noticed that the planters had very sharp corners (part of the Landscape Plan's overall angular design) and were made from brick exactly the same terracotta color as the floor paving tiles. I squinted and saw that the planters and pavers blended into each other.

If unsuspecting seniors (with declining eyesight) decide to go outside for a stroll to plant and prune, would they be able to differentiate between the same-colored planters and paving? Or would they smack their legs into a sharp planter corner? After a few smacks and aching legs would they decide that walking outside to toil the earth wasn't quite worth the pain? Probably! Who cares how many design awards a place receives if it defeats its primary purpose through color choices?

It would have been so easy for the designers to specify a contrasting color for the raised planters (tan brick planters on terra cotta colored paving tiles, for example, or a contrasting band of bricks at the base of each planter). Either strategy would have called attention to the sharp corners. (Although designing sharp corners in a place for people whose eyesight is fading seems questionable.)

> ...the core principle of ecological psychology – that a person and his or her environment aren't separate entities but form an interdependent behavior setting... a dynamic that influences how we feel and what we do.
> Roger Barker, Ecological Psychology

III. Cliffing / Centering Concept #3:

Flooring Borders can visually shift the center of a Corridor towards safety – or towards danger.

Symmetrical Borders

A 12-inch wide flooring border in a different color than the flooring field (in carpet, vinyl, rubber, tile or stone) is a very common design feature in corridors. A symmetrical border (with the same border width, material, color and texture on both sides of the corridor) will not change the perception of where the center of the corridor is. (See Figure 4.7)

But a symmetrical border could change the perceived width of the corridor, making the corridor appear narrower than it is. This could happen if the border color is closer to the wall color than it is to the floor field color.

Do the Squint Test again. If the wall appears to start at the 12-inch floor border instead of at the bottom of the wall, then the corridor would psychologically shrink 24 inches. So a 5-feet-wide corridor could visually shrink to 3 feet just because colored 12-inch borders were added for purely aesthetic reasons. This could easily trigger the same safety problems as cliffing with a large number of people trying to position their bodies in the same narrow central corridor space.

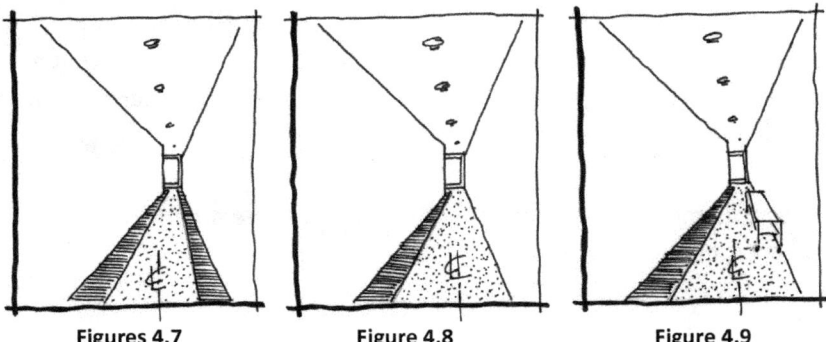

| Figures 4.7 | Figure 4.8 | Figure 4.9 |

This corridor's perceived centerline shifts depending upon border placement (a positive or negative depending upon end-user goals and space utilization)

Asymmetrical Borders

Sometimes a flooring border is located on just one side of a corridor either to add aesthetic interest or for functional purposes (like ringing a block of classrooms in a school or exam rooms in a clinic).
(See Figure 4.8)

An Asymmetrical Border can:
- Change the perceived corridor width if its color blends into the wall color. *(A 44-inch wide corridor could appear to be just 32 inches wide with one 12-inch border.)*

- Shift the perceived center of the corridor causing people to walk closer to one wall than the other. *(If the vision-impaired believe the corridor is 48 inches wide instead of 60 inches, then they might try to position themselves 24 inches from the wall instead of a safer 30 inches).* (See Figure 4.8)

An Asymmetrical Border can lead people into danger!

Since an asymmetrical border may cause people to walk closer to one wall than to the other, this isn't a good design choice if equipment or furnishings project from both walls. Walking safely in the center of an object-filled corridor is the safest strategy. Shifting the visual center of the corridor could be dangerous to some end-users if it leads them into the side of objects. (See Figure 4.9)

Does this mean that every corridor should have a continuous floor color from wall to wall?

Of course not!

Our interiors would be boring and poorly designed places if they all looked the same. As long as borders aren't located for aesthetic architectural reasons alone (that disregard potential furniture, fixtures and equipment), designers can use borders for a variety of positive and creative purposes:

IV.   Cliffing / Centering Concept #4:

You can creatively manipulate flooring borders to benefit end-users.

Since you know that flooring borders can change the perceived width and center of a corridor, here are some interesting ways to play with these ideas:

A. An Asymmetrical Border can keep people away from danger

If furniture and equipment (like metal hospital carts) are restricted to just one side of the corridor, then designing a contrasting flooring border on the corridor side below these objects will help prevent people from smashing into them.

FLOORING PSYCH • 83

Even before they reach the stretch of corridor with protruding objects, people will unconsciously walk away from the wall in the safer <u>artificial visual center</u> of the corridor. This will reduce tripping and falling. (Compare Figures 4.9 and 4.10)

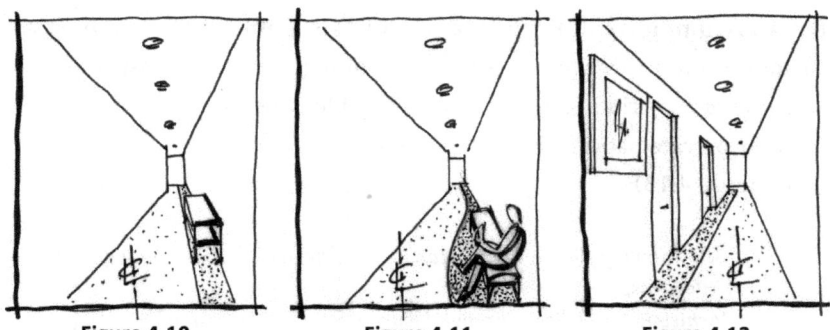

Figure 4.10   Figure 4.11   Figure 4.12
You can manipulate the corridor centerline to keep people safe and comfortable

B. <u>Asymmetrical Borders can reduce the stress of people sitting in corridors</u>

People sitting in a chair or on a bench above a wide flooring border will feel safer and more comfortable. There will be less likelihood of preoccupied cell-phone users smashing into them from the side and people won't feel like they are sitting in the middle of the corridor; YOU have purposely and wisely shifted the perceived center of the corridor <u>away</u> from them!

You can accomplish this with either a wide border in a very wide corridor or with a meandering border that expands to "support" a seating group.
(See Figure 4.11)

C. An Asymmetrical Border can help reduce doorway crashes

If doorways to highly populated rooms, suites, stores or departments are on the border side of a wide corridor, then it will be less likely that people leaving a room will bump into someone walking down the corridor, since the walkers will unconsciously position themselves <u>away</u> from the doorways. (See Figure 4.12)

D. An Asymmetrical Border can provide a public / private barrier

In addition to preventing crashes, positioning a high-contrast border on one side of a corridor can psychologically block people from "crossing" it to enter private patient rooms, offices and other spaces. (See Figure 4.13)

> *The use of varying floor materials can help define public, visitor-only and private areas in the hospital*
> "Achieving EBD Goals through Flooring Selection & Design",
> The Center for Health Design, www.healthdesign.org/chd/research

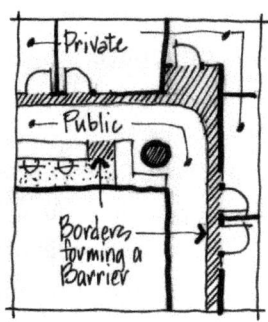

Figure 4.13
Borders can create visual barriers between the corridor, nursing stations and patient rooms

Back to nature: Think of a flooring border as a narrow stream. It's easier for people to walk alongside the stream on a path than jump over it. Those instincts still govern our unconscious behavior inside buildings.

So when you design flooring patterns, think of places where you don't want people to "cross the stream". For example, at the end of long corridors in every project type, there are often private rooms or areas (patient or guest rooms, private offices, workstations, seating areas, classrooms, etc.).

People in end-of-corridor locations often feel "on display" at the same time that someone walking straight ahead engrossed in conversation can unintentionally find himself intruding. In these cases, a high-contrast border can lead people instinctively around a corner (like following a winding riverbank) while also dividing the public corridor from private areas. (See Figure 4.13)

> Rooms should be planned with clarity of purpose. Keep spaces understandable, with public spaces very public and private spaces very private.
> Cynthia Leibrock and Debra Harris, <u>Design Details for Health</u>

E. An Asymmetrical Border can be used as a Wayfinding Tool

In large building complexes, finding your way, or wayfinding (a term most commonly used in Healthcare Facilities with miles of twisting corridors) is an increasing concern. People don't like feeling lost. That totally decreases "Patient Satisfaction"; a huge concern in healthcare today. Additionally, giving instructions to lost patients and visitors uses hundreds of hours of staff time at great cost to each healthcare facility.

> In a study conducted at a major regional 604-bed tertiary care hospital, the annual cost of the wayfinding system was calculated to be more than $220,000 per year in the main hospital, or $448 per bed per year in 1990.
> Much of this was the hidden cost of direction giving by people other than information staff, which occupied more than 4,500 staff hours, the equivalent of more than two full-time positions. (Craig Zimring, 1990)
> "A Review of the Research Literature in Evidence-Based Healthcare Design," HERD Spring 2008, VOL. 1

A flooring border can be an effective part of a wayfinding program by:

- Leading people out of a department or building.
  ("Follow the yellow border to the exit door")

- Wrapping around and identifying a popular destination.
  ("Look for the blue border and keep following it around corners until you find the Pharmacy door").

- The possibilities are endless.

V.   Cliffing / Centering Concept #5:

Don't Intentionally Blur the Boundaries...

I include many photographs in my workshops and seminars that show how designers purposely blur the boundaries between floors and vertical planes by bringing carpet, tile or wood up onto walls and millwork – or by continuing the same colors in those locations.

Sometimes this is done for a purpose like focusing attention on the merchandise in a retail store (as in the previous Monochromatic Bubble chapter examples). But often this design idea doesn't anticipate how people will actually behave. The following are real situations:

- A drugged patient stood 36 inches away from a Nurses Station vainly trying to talk to a nurse. The plastic laminate face panel of the Nurses Station and the adjacent 36-inch wide rubber flooring border were the same color brown. He was confused about where the brown flooring stopped and the brown station front started so he stood about 36 inches away from the desk (in the middle of the corridor).

- A cafeteria with bright red carpet, red chairs and red tables (but not a Monochromatic Bubble because the walls, ceilings and artwork were different colors) looks great in the design magazine. But it would look like a "sea of red" to someone with vision problems who would have trouble walking through the room without bumping into dozens of tables and chairs.

The real question is, *"Who will be eating here?"*

Luckily the red room is a college cafeteria so there probably aren't many bruised hips – just fast eaters (more on that in a later chapter).

IN THIS CHAPTER YOU LEARNED ABOUT CLIFFING AND CENTERING. NOW YOU CAN VISUALLY MANIPULATE A FLOORING BORDER IN ANY CORRIDOR FOR A VARIETY OF POSITIVE PURPOSES TO BENEFIT YOUR CLIENT.

YOU CAN ALSO HELP YOUR OWN MARKETING EFFORTS BY IDENTIFYING THOSE BENEFITS AND TELLING YOUR CLIENTS HOW <u>YOUR</u> DESIGN CAN HELP <u>THEM</u>!

> *Clients exposed to credible data on positive outcomes will be more likely to engage firms and practitioners with a record of measurable success... or may deliberately shift to those who appear to offer improved performance.*
> D. Kirk Hamilton and David H. Watkins,
> <u>Evidence Based Design for Multiple Business Types</u>

HIDDEN MESSAGE #5:

A Wind Tunnel Isn't a Safe Place for People

> *Chi, often referred to as Dragon Energy or Breath... largely invisible, made up of Sheng Chi - beneficial energy, gently meandering, found in curves and natural formations... and Sha Chi - malignant energy, viciously striking in straight lines, found in manmade formations that lack natural energy...*
> Golden Gate School of Feng Shui

IN THIS CHAPTER YOU WILL LEARN HOW LINEAR FLOORING PATTERNS AND BORDERS CAN CREATE STRESS BY ACCENTING LONG STRAIGHT CORRIDORS.

I. Energy: Visible and Invisible, Positive and Negative

In this Hidden Message I talk about energy. It's not something we normally consider when we select flooring; but shifting human energy is a direct and often unintentional result of our design decisions.

While I was studying instinct-related building practices in ancient cultures, one universal principle emerged:

Every culture around the world believed that invisible energy ran throughout Nature: heavens, earth, plants, animals and people – and that we can use that energy to improve our lives.

Our ancestors on every continent believed (very literally) that this energy needed to be balanced in order for people to live balanced lives. They recognized that the most life-supporting and bountiful environments in nature are temperate and balanced – not extreme.

This invisible energy, life force or "cosmic breath" had many names:
- In Greece this life force was called *pneuma*
- In China *chi*
- In Arabic *rouh*
- In Northern Europe *Ond, The Eight Winds or the Vital Spirit*
- In North America, the Iroquois *orenda*
- In Japan *ki*
- In India *prana*
- In Hebrew *ruach*
- In Aboriginal Australia *djang or ungud*

> *In the Northern European Tradition, the power called Ond is the driving force...the fundamental living energy of the cosmos which connects and relates all things...*
> Nigel Pennick, <u>Earth Harmony</u>

The idea that an invisible energy force flows through all of life was never abandoned in eastern civilizations – just in the western world. For the past few hundred years, the educated western man believed that if you couldn't <u>see</u> something then it didn't <u>exist</u>, (so forget all the chi, prana and ond swirling around out there).

That's the reason why doctors didn't wash their hands between patients until the late 19th century. They couldn't SEE the deadly bacteria that they were spreading from patient to patient.

> When I was born in 1895, reality was everything you could see, smell, touch and hear. The world was thought to be absolutely self-evident. When I was three years old, the electron was discovered. That was the first invisible. It didn't get in any of the newspapers. (Nobody though that would be important!) Today 99.99 percent of everything that affects our lives cannot be detected by human senses. We live in a world of invisibles.
> Buckminster Fuller

In the 20th century western educated people started believing again in the existence of invisible energy. What else are atoms, electrons, neutrons and protons?

Without invisible energy how could we:
- Lie on a couch, press a button and channel-surf?
- Sit in a coffee shop and read our e-mails?
- Text a friend after making online dinner reservations?
- Ask Siri for directions when we're lost? *(And have her <u>answer</u>?)*
- Hold a conference via speakerphone or Skype?

Destructive Rushing and Pushing Wind Tunnel Energy

Since ancient cultures believed in an invisible energy force, then it makes complete sense that they classified energy as "good or bad". Doesn't today's media constantly develop "10 Best" and "10 Worst" lists? Why would our ancestors be any different than we are?

Ancient cultures categorized the speeding energies of hurricanes, tsunamis, tornados and storms as bad energy (for totally obvious reasons). These dangerous energies share one common characteristic. They all move in long straight paths that overwhelm the helpless creatures in their way.

Wind Tunnel Energy negatively affects your 21st-century life force:

- When you find yourself driving faster and faster on a long straight highway, unaware of your speed until you look down at the speedometer and think, *"How did this happen? SLOW DOWN!"*
- Or when you ski down a Black Diamond gathering speed until your self-preservation instinct kicks in and you think, *"HELP! I'm losing control!"* before you turn your skis uphill to slow down.
- Or if friends buy a fabulous dream house on the ocean but begin to feel nervous as waves crash towards them during storms day after day after day after day…

> *If the streets run full in the face of the winds, their constant blasts rushing from the open country, and then confined by narrow alleys, will sweep through then with great violence. The lines of houses must therefore be directed away from the quarters from which the winds blow, so that as they come in they may strike against the angles of the blocks and their force thus be broken and dispersed.*
>   Vitruvius, Rome

Our explorer-ancestors knew that positioning a village at the turn of a long river could be dangerous during the rainy season when the river could roar over its banks, flooding any structure in its way.

Similarly, living at the end of a long straight road could be dangerous if horses bolted, and carts (like speeding cars today) sailed uncontrollably into buildings.

Today, homebuyers who understand Feng Shui would never buy a house located at the end of a "T" intersection where car headlights aim into windows and jangle nerves at night. That's negative "rushing chi".

> *Straight roads are especially treacherous because their shape imitates that of an arrow being shot from a bow. The arrow points directly to anything located at the end of its path. Energy naturally flows in a gentle curve. When it is forced into straight lines it tends to pick up speed. Think of a speeding bullet.*
> Angel Thompson, <u>Feng Shui</u>

People Feel Safer Slightly Off the Beaten Path

People don't feel comfortable in the middle of a strong energy path. Our natural instinct is to position ourselves someplace off to the side in a safer location where we have the opportunity to "fight or flee" if the going gets rough. Retail designers always plan corridors and displays with this instinct in mind.

> *Our research shows that women...gravitate away from the hubbub... That's how women prefer to shop; within view of the main flow of traffic, but sheltered in sectioned-off areas.*
> Paco Underhill, <u>Why We Buy</u>

Question: How is "rushing chi" related to floor patterns?

Answer: For small buildings with short corridors – it isn't. But for large building complexes with miles of corridors (or even the typical office floor) designers should recognize the floor patterns that can create this type of stress.

II. Avoid Floor Patterns that Turn Corridors into Stressful Wind Tunnels

Long straight paths do not exist in nurturing natural environments. So when a floor pattern accentuates a corridor's straightness, then we might feel uncomfortably carried along by the rushing energy. People can find themselves walking faster (just like driving faster on a straight highway). People also focus more attention on whatever is at the end of the corridor, regardless of what it is.

Question: Which floor patterns can make us move faster?
Answer: A pattern that runs parallel to the corridor.

Some Examples:
- A corridor floor pattern with a straight border in a different color, texture or material makes the corridor look even narrower and more pointed. (See Figure 4.7)
- Any linear individual flooring pattern with lines, waves, or a texture that runs parallel to the corridor length for a long distance without interruption will also create a Wind Tunnel.

Scale is important since a larger scale linear pattern magnifies the Wind Tunnel effect (especially if linear lighting, chair-rails, and other architectural features that parallel the corridor reinforce the linear floor pattern). (See Figure 5.1)

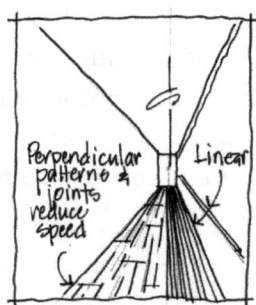

Figure 5.1:
A Linear Floor Pattern increases Speed and (potentially) Stress

Sometimes creating a Wind Tunnel effect is intentionally part of a design scheme because it feels edgy and can create an optical illusion by warping the corridor perspective. That's fine if it supports the client's purpose.

Remember that I'm not talking exclusively about the pattern, style or shape of an individual carpet, porcelain or rubber tile.

- Some linear styles create a strong overall Wind Tunnel pattern only if they are installed entirely parallel to the walls. A linear tile pattern installed in an alternating horizontal and vertical layout like quarter-turning, for example, could create a stable and balanced look.
- The effect of a small-scale linear pattern can be subtle and doesn't always produce this "rushing energy" feeling.
- Contrasting grout colors can also help prevent a Wind Tunnel effect if the tiles themselves have a linear pattern. (See Figure 5.1)
- Use the Squint Test if you have questions about the effect of a specific flooring style, shape, layout or grout color.

Question: Which floor patterns slow our movements?
Answer: A pattern that runs perpendicular to the corridor.

As Hidden Message #3 described, we instinctively perceive a line on the floor as a potential elevation change so we slow down when we unconsciously believe a plane change ahead might cause us to trip. (Figure 5.1)

Imaginary Stair Story

One client planning a renovation asked me to walk through their medical center and make recommendations. I noticed that their previous designers had attempted to break up the long corridors and alert people to department entrances using colored accent stripes about 12" wide that extended from the corridor into each Waiting Room. (See Figure 5.2)

Unfortunately the dark-colored stripes extended all the way across the corridor to the opposite wall so they looked exactly like floor treads until you were very close. That situation could too easily cause the elderly and visually impaired to trip after tensing their bodies while preparing to step up onto a non-existent stair tread.

The solution? If the designers had understood this Hidden Message, then they could have applied the same graphic design idea safely by extending the colored stripes only part way across the corridor (or in the middle of the corridor). This would still have called attention to the department entries while slowing the traffic flow. Our subconscious brains know that stair treads don't stop partway across a corridor. These accent floor strips would have "read" as what they actually were (just a colored accent graphic) without creating the possibility of tensing and tripping. (See Figure 5.3)

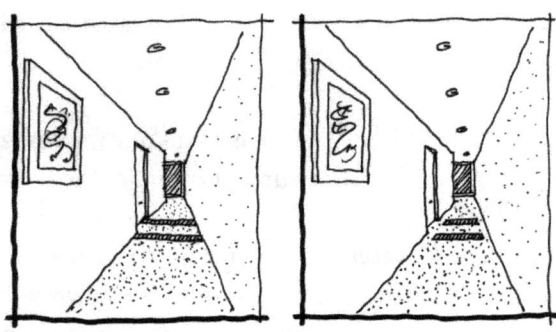

Figure 5.2   **Figure 5.3**
Stairs or Flooring Accent Features? What's Up Ahead?

Break up the Highway by Changing the Road Surface

> ...distances judged along a horizontal surface seem shorter when a discontinuity in the surface is produced by using two different surface textures (pattern designs), the same pattern with the contrasts reversed, or the same pattern with a horizontal offset.
>   (Feria, Braunstein and Anderson, 2004)

Another way to reduce one long tunnel into a series of more comfortable smaller spaces is to change the flooring color, material, pattern or texture. This works particularly well in places where changing the floor pattern is part of the facility's wayfinding strategy.

- A floor change at the intersection between two corridors will alert people where they might encounter another fast-moving person or may need to make a decision about where to go next.

- A floor change can help identify distant Rest Rooms, Elevators and other popular destinations.
  ("See that green floor up ahead? The Rest Rooms are to the right.")

- A floor change at the entries to apartments, hotel and patient rooms, office suites, and departments in large organizations can begin the transition from public to private space (much like a doormat or potted plant at a residential front door).

You can develop your own ideas for how to safely break the flow with perpendicular designs. But remember to just select lower contrast and monochromatic floor colors and patterns if the corridor is short and you only want people to slow down slightly. The stronger the contrast, the slower some people will walk (unconsciously expecting plane changes like the Grandmother in Chapter 3).

III. Floor Patterns Can Create Stress for People Sitting at the End of the Tunnel

Since people often look straight ahead while walking, whatever is at the end of a long corridor will get even more attention when a linear floor pattern leads feet and eyes in that direction.

If you can't change an unattractive view at the end of a long corridor, then you may need to create distractions by breaking up the flooring with color or pattern changes.

The Importance of Privacy and Control

If people will be sitting at the end of a long corridor in a workstation or seating group, then a linear floor pattern will make them feel even more uncomfortably "on display". That situation violates our instinctive and universal preference for Privacy and Control.

> *Privacy is intimately connected to our sense of control or autonomy. The ability to choose solitude or the company of others endows us with a sense of self-determination: not having that choice makes us feel helpless...*
> Allyn and Bacon, <u>Environmental Psychology Principles and Practice</u>

IV. Design action steps you can use to avoid creating stressful wind tunnel corridors

Action Step #1:

Imagine you've stepped into Charlie's Chocolate Factory's Miniaturization Machine. Now pretend that you are walking down every corridor shown on your Floor Plan. What do you see at the end of each corridor? How will this view make you feel if you are lost, just argued with your boss, or are having a 'bad hair' day?

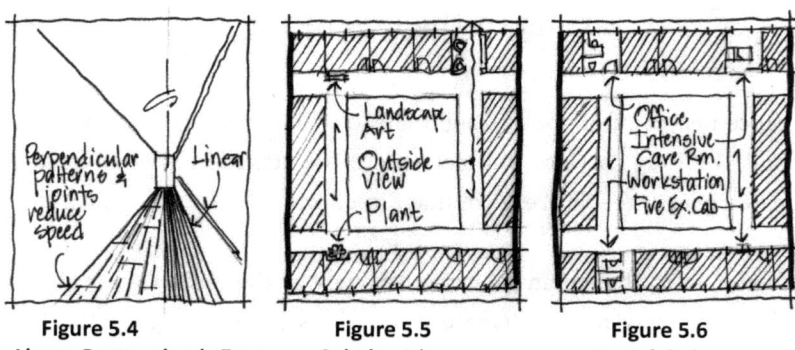

Figure 5.4
Linear Pattern leads Eyes

Figure 5.5
Calming Views

Figure 5.6
Stressful Views

- **A window with a wonderful nature view?**
  (Great for calming nerves, according to research studies)

  Neuroscience research, with functional MRI's, has confirmed that viewing natural environments reduces stress and helps us return to productivity after we've become mentally exhausted by doing work that requires concentration
      (Kim et al., 2010)

- **A lush landscape painting illuminated by soft lighting?**
  (Almost as good as a window)

  Looking at simulated nature views can reduce stress... when intake officers at a county jail had a view of a large-scale photomural of a nature scene, they experienced less stress during their shifts than when the mural was absent
      (Farbstein et al., 2012)

- **A tall thriving green plant?**   (Good)

  Live plants in an office, even without window views, lead to more positive psychological states.
      (Dravigne)

- **A fire extinguisher cabinet?**   (Uneasy)
  "Will I ever need that? How would I get out of here if there *is* a fire?"

- **A Toilet Room door?**   (Even worse)
  No one ever felt happier or healthier thinking about toilets.
  (See Figures 5.5 and 5.6 for sketches of the previous examples)

Action Step #2:

Pretend you are sitting or working in the area or room at the end of each long corridor.

- **A Private Office or Guest Room?**   (Unsettling)

This is psychologically not a comfortable place for the inhabitant who experiences more unexpected visitors and feels that he or she has less privacy. Additionally, more noise from the corridor will tumble into this room. Often my corporate clients realize that their offices at the end of corridors experience higher turnover - after I ask that question.

- **An Open Workstation?**   (There goes staff retention)

Staff turnover in end-of-corridor workstations is even worse since the staff member will feel fully exposed despite high plants and furniture panels acting as barricades. The voices of people heading directly towards a station will make that occupant feel especially anxious.

- **A Glass-Walled Conference Room?**   (Distracting)

For the attendees sitting at the table, having people walk directly towards them throughout a meeting may reduce productivity and the ability to focus on the conversation or task at hand.

- **A Glass-Walled Intensive Care Patient Room**?   (Deadly)

The first time I consulted on a healthcare project, I was the Feng Shui Consultant. A member of the hospital's Board of Directors (who was interested in eastern philosophy and also recognized that there would be a large percentage of Asian staff and patients in the hospital) brought me onto the project team. So I reviewed floor plans and found a glass-walled ICU room at the end of a very long corridor.

Use your imagination and pretend you are the poor car crash victim lying in an Intensive Care bed connected to tubes and monitors.

You wake up, look up through your glass wall and see dozens of people walking towards you and (seemingly) <u>LOOKING DIRECTLY AT YOU</u> while they walk down the 200-foot long corridor.
Some are even <u>RUNNING TOWARDS YOU</u> before they make 90-degree turns into other ICU rooms.

That would be enough to give you a heart attack on top of your other problems! So due to your room assignment, your survival rate might be lower due to increased stress and anxiety than another patient tucked safely off to the side of the corridor (the position those healthy shoppers in the retail studies prefer).

Fortunately when I brought this to the attention of the Medical Planner, he immediately switched the Clean Linen Room to the end of the corridor. Looking at a "Clean Linen" sign while walking down the corridor would be fine - not as good as viewing landscape artwork but far better than seeing a "Soiled Linen" sign!

(See Figure 5.6 for a sketch of the previous stressful examples)

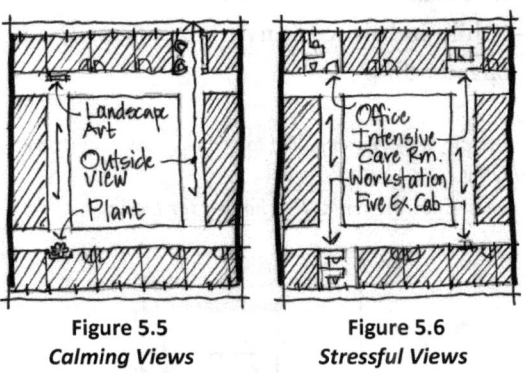

Figure 5.5
Calming Views

Figure 5.6
Stressful Views

Action Step #3:

Pretend you are entering a short corridor or a small room with a bold linear floor stripe headed... wherever.

Running a large stripe of a single color tile or carpet into a wall in a small room (like an Exam or Patient Room) seems to be very popular in healthcare design today. Is this because the large single stripe looks different than designs in the past - back to "novelty"?

If your eyes follow the stripe to its end (which automatically happens) then you might see something the designer did not anticipate:

- A chair sitting partially on and partially off the stripe.
- Artwork, signage or medical devices not centered on the stripe or even the edge of the stripe - just located randomly in obviously uncoordinated locations (See Figure 5.7)

It would be fine if there were an aesthetically pleasing purpose (or any describable purpose) in creating wide random floor stripes. But unless they are coordinated with furniture or artwork placement, the resulting imbalanced design will just feel jarring and chaotic to most end-users. Studies show that balanced and symmetrical environments reduce stress and energy – while imbalanced environments do the opposite. (More about that in Chapter 8).

> *Law of Symmetry: We are compelled to group dissimilar items together so as to create symmetry.*
> Dak Kopec, <u>Environmental Psychology for Design</u>

Figure 5.7
This floor stripe creates imbalance and adds to the clutter

> *The Vedic law of nature sees an innate order and harmony in the universe. Nothing man-made should interfere with this governing principle.*
> Kathleen Cox, <u>Vastu Living</u>

Additionally (getting back to the fact that people feel more comfortable in environments that remind them of familiar residential settings), there is nothing about a large stripe ramming into a wall that would remind people of home or a pleasant hotel experience – no positive memory-joggers.

> In one ward, the reflection on the floor tile from a row of lights gave the impression of a highway with a white stripe down the center.
> "Floor Designs Can Be Therapeutic", Robert Sommer

Okay – unplanned and slightly uncomfortable isn't deadly. But designing with one large stripe or another bold linear pattern that is not coordinated with other interior design features like lighting and furniture might be another case of "because we can" and not "because we should".

IN THIS CHAPTER YOU LEARNED TO IDENTIFY THE FLOORING PATTERNS THAT CREATE AN UNCOMFORTABLE WIND TUNNEL EFFECT FOR MOST PEOPLE.

If accenting the linear form of long interior corridors doesn't feel instinctively comfortable to people outside the design profession, then what floor patterns will feel instinctively comfortable? That brings us to the next Hidden Message based upon nature and instinct (and the photograph on the cover of this book):

Organic isn't just a Food Label –
We all like following a Meandering Path.

> Among the Zulus there is no word for, and no real concept of straight lines, square and rectangle. Theirs is a world of round doors and windows and villages laid out in circles... a non-carpentered world.
> Ittelson, Proshansky, Rivlin and Winkel,
> An Introduction to Environmental Psychology

HIDDEN MESSAGE #6:

Organic isn't just a Food Label – We all like following a Meandering Path

NOW THAT YOU UNDERSTAND THE NEGATIVE IMPACT OF WIND TUNNEL CORRIDORS, THIS CHAPTER WILL HELP YOU PROPOSE APPROPRIATE CURVING FLOOR PATTERNS TO INCREASE COMFORT

Organic, adj. (Latin: organicus)
Exhibiting characters peculiar to living organisms, like animals and plants...
(and people)

I.   Curving Land Formations (and bodies)

Picture Conan or Ayla walking through fields and forests around a hill or following the banks of a winding river the way our ancestors did for hundreds of thousands of years. Their paths curved gently from one group of huts to another (like the forest path on the cover of this book). Those huts turned into villages, and later, towns and cities – all connected by curving, meandering paths. Some ancient walkways became the winding roads and alleyways in the oldest sections of Paris, Rome, London and the other great cities of the world that we love visiting.

> *In the days of hand-power it was easier to go round a tree-root or a boulder or follow a contour than go straight through. The lines that resulted – for path, field boundary or building placement were... in conversation with the landscape... Powerful machinery finds it easier to disregard the irregularities of the surroundings...*
>   Christopher Day, <u>Places of the Soul</u>

The Great Wall of China perfectly represents this principle. It has stood for thousands of years, following the earth's curves and contours. Its planners and builders believed that cutting through the "earth dragon" shapes created by hills and mountains would damage the energy of the natural environment and would cause great harm to their Empire.

Geomancy is the inclusive name for all the earth sciences. It stems from "Gaia" (the Greek goddess personifying the earth) and "manteia" (meaning oracle or divination). Geomancy teaches that places with hills and winding rivers (which create smoothly flowing energy) are the best places for people. Not coincidentally, those features existed in the places that ancient cultures chose to safely locate their earliest settlements (within the bends of the Seine River in Paris, the Thames in London and the Tiber in Rome among thousands of others throughout the world).

Nude Model Story (a tenuous connection to flooring)

It wasn't just landscape features that influenced the creation of meandering paths. Human physiology prevented our ancestors (and prevents us today) from walking in a straight line from Point A to Point B. Nature is made up of curves and people are, too (as anyone who has ever taken a drawing class and attempted to paint a nude model knows - a very bizarre and self-conscious experience, initially).

As an Art Major, in my first drawing class with a live model, I remember all of us students surrounding a naked girl with a lot of goose bumps. (It <u>was</u> chilly Madison, Wisconsin.) I can still hear the frustrated art professor yelling and gesturing wildly since we were all drawing very small precise images in chalk,

"Curves! BIG CURVES! Do you SEE any straight lines?
Even if you're just drawing her arm or her foot.
NO STRAIGHT LINES!!! FILL THE PAPER WITH BIG CURVES!!!"

College Campus in the Snow Story (a less tenuous connection to flooring)

Our instinctive tendency to veer right or left as we walk is obvious when you look at a college campus after a snowfall. The straight paved walkways and 90-degree turns that connect the academic buildings around a quadrangle have been obliterated. Instead, the students' trampling boots have created large curving paths connecting the buildings.

> *...without external cues to direction, people trying to walk straight over unfamiliar terrain end up doing intermittent loop-de-loops. Researchers observed these circular routes when people were walking in fairly sparse environments, such as the Sahara Desert, but also when they were traveling through densely wooded areas.*
> Bruce Bower, "How to Walk in Circles without Really Trying."
> *Science News*, 2009

Retail researcher Paco Underhill noted in his book Why We Buy: The Science of Shopping that people generally drift unconsciously to the right. Even people who are purposely walking from one store to another swerve slightly as their energy is attracted to a bright color here or the smell of Cinnamon Buns there.

> *The smart store, then, is designed in accordance with how we walk and where we look. It understands our habits of movement and takes advantage of them, rather than ignoring them or, even worse, trying to change them.*
> Paco Underhill, Why We Buy

Studies show that in countries where we drive on the right side of the road, people tend to start out veering towards the right. We enter a grocery store through the doors farthest right, for example, heading even further right inside the store and then winding back toward the left side of the store. Typically, supermarkets, department stores and retail shops are purposely planned to accommodate this instinct in order to increase their sales by locating specific products in specific places.

The same happens in reverse in countries where people drive on the left side of the road. (In the time before driving and in the few places on earth where cars don't rule, studies show that people favor starting to the right, perhaps because the majority of people are right-handed.)

II.   How do You Design Floor Patterns to Reinforce our Meandering Instincts?

A.   Where possible, literally curve corridors and pathways.

This is obviously easier to do with exterior paving that curves gently (emphasis on the word "gently"). We don't instinctively zigzag or veer sharply from one side to the other. Curving architectural features and paths need to feel natural – not forced. (See Figure 6.1)

> ...circular paths minimize disorientation and fear of getting lost. Recent research indicates that paths that travel through garden areas or even along corridors with much shadowing or mottling...seem to have a calming effect on dementia sufferers.
> Dak Kopec, *Environmental Psychology for Design*

A sharply curving walkway will feel as unnatural and uncomfortable to us as a long straight walkway. So use common sense and instinct to determine how many curves are too many curves.

A few years ago I worked with Ellerbe/AECOM and HPS Architects as a Consultant when they designed the new San Leandro Medical Center in Northern California. The Medical Center had two main entrances and a design problem: the entrance closest to the majority of the parking lots led to the Medical Office Building instead of to the larger Hospital.

There needed to be one large and very obvious corridor leading people from the MOB Entrance to the Hospital Entrance (hundreds of feet apart) without their wandering into the miles of intersecting corridors and creating a wayfinding nightmare for patients, visitors and staff.

I suggested that the architects design one wide smoothly curving corridor connecting the two entrances, so people would just naturally follow the curve. The designers embraced this idea and pushed it much further with colored curving soffits, carpet patterns, benches and sculptural pieces along the way.

Their design clearly differentiates this main connecting corridor from all the other 90-degree-corner corridors. This curving corridor successfully leads people instinctively where they need to go while adding a dramatic feeling to the Medical Center that people find comfortable and compelling. (See Figure 6.2)

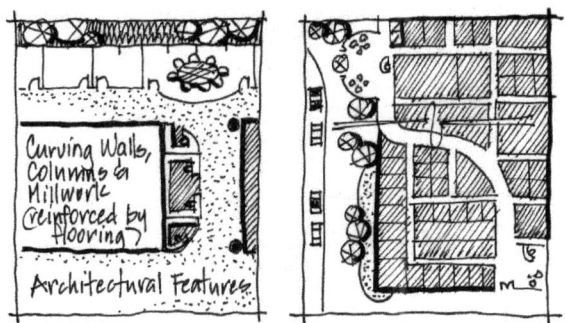

Figure 6.1   Figure 6.2
Architectural Features creating Meandering Paths

B.   You can combine different colors or patterns to create a gently curving path inside a long straight corridor.

Imagine that building corridors and hallways are the "roads and rivers" inside our 21st-century buildings.

> *A successfully conceived corridor or hallway can become a subtle metaphor for a meandering path or a flowing river. Our subconscious, in turn, can translate this experience into a sense of security and belonging, as the materials, textures and colors of these spaces remind us of primary experiences in nature.*
> Alex Stark, Feng Shui Consultant

You can help corridors feel more comfortable and meandering when your design:

- Winds a floor color or pattern from one side of the corridor to the other inside a different field (color or pattern) over a long distance. (See Figure 6.3)
- Includes gently curving accent shapes and colors.
  (See Figure 6.4)
- Establishes an alternating rhythm coordinated with architectural features along the corridor.
  (See Figure 6.5)

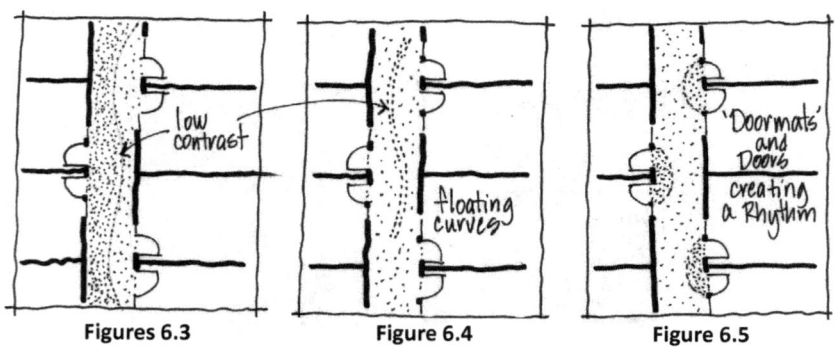

Figures 6.3   Figure 6.4   Figure 6.5

Some Floor Patterns can create comfortably Meandering Paths.
Use your imagination to develop patterns appropriate for your projects.

C.   Since people don't pivot 90 degrees at corridor intersections, you can create floor patterns that curve around corners.
This can be as simple as a contrasting carpet or tile accent feature close to the width of a path in nature (or a series of smaller colored strips creating this width) that curves around a corner at an important corridor intersection. (See Figure 6.7)

We unconsciously follow pathways (natural or artificial) the width that our ancestors followed through the wilderness - a few feet. If our attention is automatically drawn along the path and around the corner (instead of into the room ahead), then our feet will follow. The next chapter will describe more about using this instinct in a wayfinding program.

Think of any other metaphor from nature that wraps around corners, like stepping-stones across a winding stream. (See Figure 6.8) I recommended this concept to the Interior Designers of the Medical Center and they designed a "bamboo stick" pattern using multiple colors of vinyl flooring that create meandering corridors while leading people around corners, into specific rooms, and satisfy other functional purposes throughout the enormous Hospital and MOB complex.
(See Figure 6.6)

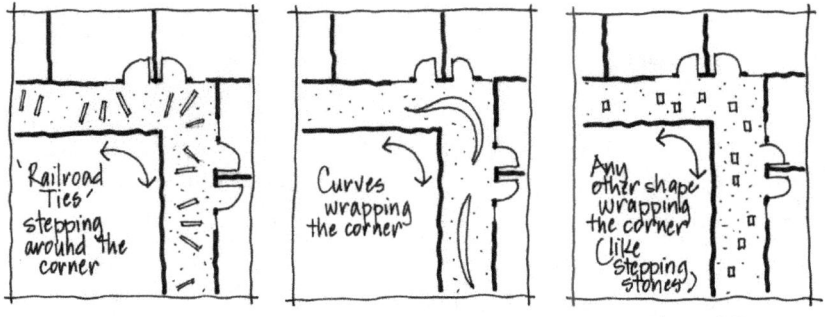

Figures 6.6   **Figure 6.7**   **Figure 6.8**
Floor Patterns that lead people instinctively around corners

D. You can visually expand a long straight corridor into an adjacent room or area so it appears to widen and narrow (like a river onto a riverbank, or a forest path expanding into a clearing).
Often there is an Open Office Workstation Area, a Glass Walled Conference Room, a Waiting Room or a Seating Area adjacent to a Corridor and you can "borrow space" visually. Continue the corridor flooring and wall finishes into this room or area (instead of changing colors or patterns) to create an overall meandering feeling when a long corridor must remain perfectly rectilinear.
(See Figure 6.9)

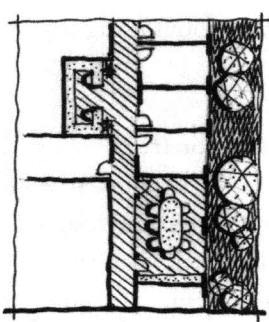

Figure 6.9
"Expanding" a corridor by extending flooring into adjacent spaces

> *Hallways and lobbies can remind us of glens or eddies, and when combined with conscious approaches to architectural volumes, window and wall configurations, can begin to bio-mimic our experiences in the natural world.*
>   Alex Stark, Feng Shui Consultant

E. You can incorporate curvilinear features: circles, arcs or representational figures like arching dolphins (as one airport did) within your floor pattern.
This design strategy is used frequently in large rectangular hospitality rooms and long wide corridors like those in airports. Curving floor patterns, forms and shapes reduce the rigid feeling, especially if ceiling soffits, other architectural features and specifically placed artwork and

lighting create a rhythm that reinforces the curving floor patterns (and vice versa).

Studies show that people feel more relaxed in places with curves.

> In general, objects and patterns with curved features are preferred to those with pointed features and sharp angles. Research has shown that we associate circles with softness, happiness, goodness, love, life, brightness, lightness, warmth, quickness and quietness.
> Sally Augustin PhD,
> Place Advantage: Applied Psychology for Interior Architecture

KTVU / Cox Media Group's "Where's the Water?" Story

My Oakland client asked me to help them renovate their large second floor with new carpet, paint colors and workstations. KTVU's existing space had solid-colored carpet with workstations laid out diagonally across the Open Office Area. The diagonal workstation layout meant that everyone stepping out of the elevator (about 100 feet from the windows) and anyone walking down the primary interior corridors looked into a wall of workstations – instead of out the windows at a beautiful view of the San Francisco Bay.

KTVU has waterfront property, but only a small number of people in private offices and in the workstations directly adjacent to the windows could see the water!

I knew that in this case we needed to create a series of long corridors from the perimeter windows to the elevator and primary interior corridor. Then the 60 staff members could experience the amazing nature views whenever they stepped out of their workstations. Those would be just the type of wind tunnel corridors I generally try to avoid creating - but the stress-reducing water views were too special to ignore. In this case curving architectural elements wouldn't be possible or desirable so I needed to select a meandering carpet pattern. (See Figure 6.10)

Since energy speeds up when it travels in a straight line, it helps if any long passage has some means of slowing the energy down.
   Bilkis Whelan, <u>Vastu in 10 Simple Lessons</u>

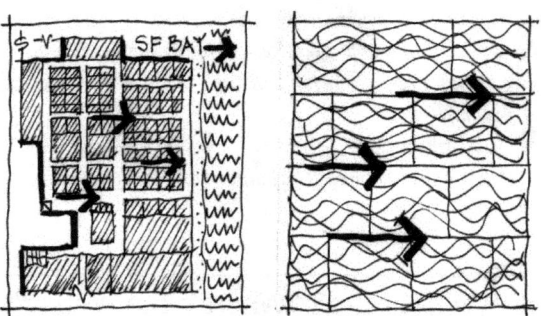

Figure 6.10   Figure 6.11
Carpet tile waves leading eyes and feet to the San Francisco Bay

Going back to client goals; I knew that the primary purpose of KTVU (the FOX Affiliate Station in Northern California) is communication. Due to the building's location and following the ancient belief that the element *WATER* can be used in design to facilitate communication (water flows just like writing, ideas and conversation flow), I proposed both blue and wavy-patterned carpet tiles (both would work for *WATER* energy – more about that in the next book).

The General Manager selected a taupe carpet tile with a very strong wave pattern that we installed in an ashlar tile layout so any visible horizontal "slow down the energy" seams were not continuous. The waves lead down the corridors toward the windows and the water – exactly where we want the attention and eyes of people who work in the dark and deep interior space (at stressful jobs) to go.
(See Figure 6.11)

Now every time I walk into KTVU someone tells me that they feel like they are working in a different building: one that was transported to Bay-front property.

So if it feels more comfortable for us to drift and curve, then why are we constantly forced into straight streets, sidewalks and corridors?
Thank economics and (in the USA) Thomas Jefferson!

> The grid that dominates much of the North American landscape remains a legacy of Thomas Jefferson. The American landscape was parceled like a large chessboard. Americans inherited a division of the land, rational in eighteenth-century views, that is incongruent with natural processes and, from an ecological point of view, irrational.
> Frederick Steiner, Human Ecology

Straight lines are much easier to draw on paper and create on CAD. Rectilinear buildings are less expensive to construct using modern building materials like 4' x 8' sheets of wall board and identically sized concrete blocks. So straight lines shape our modern world. This is especially true in the United States, where many counties and towns were planned using rectilinear grids that disregarded topographical features long before their future citizens stepped off the ships that carried new immigrants to America.

Fortunately, Healing Gardens and landscaped paths through gardens, parks and parking lots are increasingly designed to curve gently.

III. How can you easily balance sharp-cornered metal and glass buildings?

(You won't be surprised that my answer is "Floor Patterns!")
Often, as either an Architectural Design Psychology Consultant, or a Feng Shui Consultant (depending upon my client's viewpoint), I'm asked to join a project design team after most of the building has already been designed. One building owner recently asked me to make Feng Shui design recommendations that would make his new 39-story San Francisco apartment building more appealing to potential Asian tenants.

The predominantly metal and glass, grey and white high-rise building had already been submitted for a Building Permit and the building exterior was full of dramatic sharp corners and angles. The early paving and landscaping plans reinforced this theme with sharp-cornered stepping rectangular planters sitting on rectangular pavers at the entrances, on patios and in the pool area.

Even the pool recliners were evenly spaced in straight rows. The carpet and tile patterns, shapes and layout inside the building (in both the public and private spaces) also reinforced the overall rectilinear and angular design.

From the Feng Shui perspective (as well as current research studies) angles and corners make people feel less comfortable than curvilinear (back to Conan looking for a nice un-threatening spot in the cave away from creepy dark corners and sharp-pointed rocks).

> *People prefer "objects with a curved contour compared with objects that have pointed features and a sharp-angled contour"; and the latter triggers a response in the fear center of the brain, the amygdala.*
> *(Bar and Neta, 2007)*

Reviewing the plans and elevations, even though they showed a very high and consistent design quality, I thought that all the primarily gray, white and metal materials creating straight lines made the building look and feel more like an Office Building for serious-minded workers than a place where potential tenants (from any country) would want to relax and call "home".

There seemed to be nothing gentle, residential or organic-feeling about this building – until I came to the rooftop Dog Park Plan.
(See Figure 6.12)

Nothing rigid and tense about the Dog Park! Irregularly sized plants and trees! Pavers forming huge curving steps around circular green grass berms! Curving benches where dog owners can sit and talk while watching their frolicking pets!

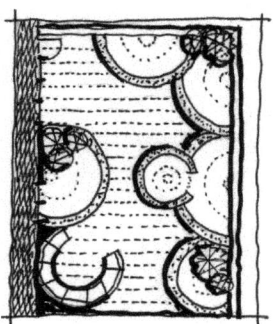

Figure 6.12
High energy in the Dog Park for people and pets

No greys here – just rich peach and terracotta colors with green grass, plants and trees. Most people would find it more fun hanging out in the curvy colorful Dog Park than anywhere else in the entire building. This space could unintentionally become the social "heart" of the entire apartment complex.

Since it was too late for me to recommend changes to architectural features, I focused my exterior recommendations on paving, landscape forms, planters and plants on the ground floor, the pool area and on multiple upper-floor patios and decks of public spaces. Many of my interior recommendations also related to creating meandering organic floor designs with more richly colored tile and carpet patterns.

Wherever possible, throughout the entire building I recommended turning the regular into the irregular, the straight into the curvy, and the grey into the colorful.

My advice (which I offer to anyone trying to increase the psychological appeal of sharp-pointed metal and glass buildings - a style much beloved by Creative Innovation-Based 21st century designers) sounded a lot like my frustrated Art Professor's instructions as we grouped self-consciously around the shivering model,

"Curves! BIG CURVES!

<u>FILL</u> THE PAPER WITH CURVES!"

IN THIS CHAPTER YOU LEARNED THAT CURVING AND MEANDERING FLOOR PATTERNS GO A LONG WAY TOWARD BALANCING ALL THE WIND TUNNEL CORRIDORS, STRAIGHT LINES AND HARD ANGLES IN 20th and 21st- CENTURY BUILDINGS.

> *... after having people look at images of rooms containing either primarily rectilinear or primarily curvilinear furniture... the curvilinear settings elicited higher amounts of pleasant, un-arousing emotions (such as feeling relaxed, peaceful, and calm) than the rectilinear settings.*
>   *(Dazkir and Read, 2012)*

HIDDEN MESSAGE #7:

Brains and Feet are Related:
I.   Sometimes our Brains follow our Feet (Pathways)
II. Sometimes our Feet follow our Brains (Landmarks)

IN THIS CHAPTER YOU WILL LEARN WAYFINDING STRATEGIES USING FLOORING PATTERNS THAT WILL HELP PEOPLE FIND THEIR WAY AROUND LARGE BUILDING COMPLEXES.

> *Linking place and territory, wayfinding describes the mental and physical activities associated with finding the way to food and potential mates, avoiding predators, and getting home to safety. The ability to find our way also helps us explore new territories, survive when our food sources have dried up, read cues from others who wish us to follow, and negotiate new and urgent situations such as hospital admissions.*
>
> John Zeisel, <u>Inquiry by Design</u>

Wayfinding is a huge concern for healthcare organizations since the number of hours that staff members spend giving directions to lost patients and visitors translates directly into lost dollars and decreased patient satisfaction.

> *In a study conducted at a major regional 604-bed tertiary care hospital, the annual cost of the wayfinding system was calculated to be more than $220,000 per year in the main hospital, or $448 per bed per year in 1990. Much of this was the hidden cost of direction giving by people other than information staff, which occupied more than 4,500 staff hours, the equivalent of more than two full-time positions.*
>
>   (Craig Zimring, 1990)

I. Instinctive Wayfinding Strategy #1: Sometimes our Brains follow our Feet (Pathways)

One human instinct relating to the environment is that we unconsciously follow paths leading in the same general direction we're walking. In nature, it's always easier and safer for people to follow a path made by animals or other people. After other feet have compacted and flattened the earth we are less likely to:
- Slip on loose dirt.
- Step into holes.
- Be scratched by prickly plants and shrubs.

So if a floor stripe or curve (inside or outside) is about as wide as the paths through the forests or fields that our ancestors followed (about 2 to 4 feet wide so people can put both feet on it), then our feet take over. We unthinkingly walk on a wide stripe when it goes in the same general direction we think we want to travel.

> *Every kind of behavior results from the way in which our minds interact with our environments... Natural selection has programmed human development to be contingent on various environmental triggers...*
> Dylan Evans and Oscar Zarate, Introducing Evolutionary Psychology

Airline Terminal Story

Last year I stood on a mezzanine bridge overlooking the new American Airline terminal in San Francisco. The ticketing area was a vast expanse of terrazzo below me – all shades of white and light grey with one medium grey terrazzo stripe about 4 feet wide heading down the length of the 40-foot-wide terminal. People walking in either direction could have positioned their bodies anywhere within that 40 foot width – but where did most people head? Toward the darker stripe.

Their feet took off and their brains followed. There wasn't any rational reason to walk on the darker stripe. But person after person pulled their rolling bags along that one darker stripe until they met someone coming in the opposite direction and one person was forced to step "off".

Nobody told those dozens of people I saw, *"Step onto the dark grey stripe!"* Travelers unconsciously identified it as the only place that looked like a grounded "path" heading through the sea of white and light grey stripes and shapes, and they instinctively wanted to be on it. (See Figure 7.1)

Since brains follow feet onto stripes and curves, your flooring design can lead people where you want them to go as part of your wayfinding strategy:
- From the Main Entrance to the Elevator Bank.
- From the Elevator Bank to the Cafeteria.
- From a Classroom to the Multi-Purpose Room.
- From the Healthcare Clinic to the Pharmacy.
- Wherever you and your client want the majority of people to go in order to reduce confusion and wasted staff hours.

Changes in the environment change the brain and therefore they change our behavior. Architectural design changes our brain and our behavior.
  Rusty Gage, Salk Institute Neuroscientist, AIA Convention Keynote 2003

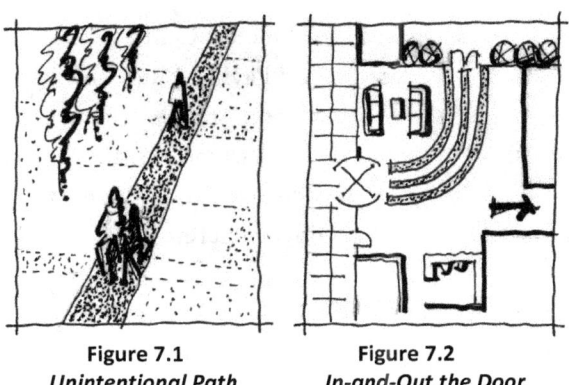

Figure 7.1
Unintentional Path

Figure 7.2
In-and-Out the Door

But brains also follow feet onto stripes and curves that lead people where we <u>don't</u> want them to go! A few examples:

"In One Door and Out the Other" Story

Prior to my leading a Wayfinding Workshop at an architectural firm that was trying to develop an instinctive circulation system in an existing building complex with a tortured corridor system, I toured medical office buildings looking for flooring examples. In one building lobby, I walked through the revolving doors at the Main Entrance and found myself on three long, brightly colored curves. The curves led from the revolving doors, around the Lounge Seating Group (which it framed nicely) and directly out the side doors leading to a small dead-end courtyard with some nice trees – but without a reason for anyone to visit!

I sat on a lounge chair and watched three people walk through the revolving doors, follow the curve about fifteen feet, slow down, correct themselves, and then switch directions to walk toward the elevator lobby. I don't think <u>that</u> was part of anybody's design strategy!
(See Figure 7.2. The arrow points to the elevator and main corridor.)

Exterior "Ouch! Crunch! And GET ME OUT OF HERE" Stories

While I was on the San Leandro Medical Center project team, I also reviewed the exterior Landscape and Paving Plans. On the first version of those plans, the Landscape Architect showed the same bamboo stick shapes (that I described in a previous chapter) since the project was well coordinated from inside to outside. This time the bamboo sticks would be made from paving tiles or stained concrete.

But the Landscaper hadn't attended my Design with a Purpose workshop, so his first paving plan was essentially a graphic design exercise (which often happens when Creative Innovation-Based brains swing into action). The bamboo sticks were used purely as graphic design shapes (instead of a purposely-designed way to lead people from the parking lots into the Main Entrance – avoiding other entries). I identified the problem areas by imagining my vulnerable Avatar walking out of Charlie's Chocolate Factory Miniaturization Machine *(Is this starting to sound familiar?)* onto the Paving Plan.

Ethel got out of her rusty white '97 Ford Explorer and followed every implied pathway on the plan with Ed in order to identify problem areas:

- Where an unintentional bamboo stick path led Ethel directly into the sharp corner of a planter (OUCH!)

- When the bamboo sticks led Ethel to the curb at the main Hospital Drop-off Zone where she and Ed bumped into a patient getting out of a car (CRUNCH!) (See Figure 7.3)

- Where the bamboo sticks led into a weirdly shaped corner between two planters. Distracted Ethel (whose attention was on getting grouchy Ed inside) thought, *"What are we doing HERE?"*

Even though the bamboo sticks were just a different color than the field paving and people could decide to walk elsewhere; this was a medical center. A number of people would be elderly, vision-impaired or just distracted by cell phones. They would unconsciously (or consciously) interpret the series of bamboo sticks as a path due to their size and shape which looked like the railroad ties that are frequently used to define steps in garden (or symbolically - lead trains from one place to another).

In his second version, the landscape designer turned his paving layout from a subjective graphic design exercise into an effective wayfinding strategy. Ethel and Ed moved smoothly and instinctively along the bamboo stick / railroad tie pathways that led from the distant parking lots to the main hospital entrance.

 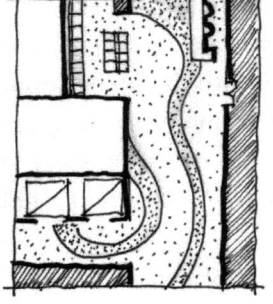

Figure 7.3
Dangerous Drop-off Zone

Figure 7.4
Paths into Walls, Desk & Column

Interior "Ouch! Crunch! And GET ME OUT OF HERE" Stories

One hospital I toured with a client was obviously designed by someone who understood the importance of using curvilinear forms to break up the geometry of straight miles-long corridors. Large colorful carpet curves swept through the corridors and broke up the wind tunnels, creating much more interesting spaces than the typical bland hospital corridors.

Unfortunately, the curves were the width of pathways and led people:
- Smack into walls.
- Into doors that said "Do Not Enter!"
- Directly into the side of a huge column.
- Into the corner of a Waiting Room Reception Desk. (See Figure 7.4)

If the designer had recognized that people unconsciously follow curves the size of a forest path, then he or she could easily have shifted the purpose of the carpet pattern - from a graphic design to a wayfinding path:

- One curve could have led people from the Elevator Lobby down the long corridor into a Waiting Room (instead of a wall)

- Another curve could have lead people into the queue line at the Reception Desk instead of into its sharp corner.

How is a Floor Pattern Typically Designed?

Designers generally create floor patterns as part of an overall design scheme that includes colors, materials and finishes on walls, ceilings and other architectural features. Schematic design decisions are generally made by designers and their clients by reviewing a colored plan that shows the flooring patterns on an entire floor.

Often this floor finishes plan includes architectural features like walls, doorways and columns, and labels room functions, but doesn't show furniture (which might be the responsibility of an entirely different group of designers). After reading descriptions of the previous Hidden Messages, you understand the importance of looking at the flooring and furniture design simultaneously – because that is how end-users will experience the space.

Another disconnect occurs because future occupants will only see one room or space at a time. They will never view the floor pattern the same way the designers and clients do. End-users would never know, for example, that a large, colored carpet, vinyl, rubber or terrazzo curve hitting a wall in one location will emerge smoothly and elegantly around the corner. It may have looked great on the plan, but end-users will only see a big curve ramming into a wall for no reason.

The only way an occupant could ever see a full floor design the same way clients do during design meetings would be if the roof blew off the building and they hovered over the building in a helicopter. Not likely...

But that is the way we typically design floor patterns – without avatars or imaginary miniaturization machines.

II. Instinctive Wayfinding Strategy #2: Sometimes our Feet Follow our Brains (Landmarks)

> *Cognitive science has uncovered cue recognition information that designers can apply... physical cues located below eye level are more readily processed...than those located above it... Gazzaniga (1998) believes this trait has evolved from our need to track our prey for food, with our ancestors being more likely to find tracks of prey and lurking predators on the ground... than up in the trees.*
> John Zeisel, <u>Inquiry by Design</u>

This section describes how we can consciously and purposely design flooring Landmarks that help lead us to our destination. Hansel (half of the famous combo Hansel and Gretel) wasn't able to follow a pathway back home. Instead he dropped breadcrumbs so he could look for them and re-trace his steps. Hansel's brain did the leading as he looked ahead for Landmarks, and his feet did the following.

> *Lost people are endemic in healthcare environments. Environments that are more cue rich, including, for example, more clear and memorable landmarks (such as color changes on walls or distinctive artwork), help people give and remember directions as well as learn and remember where they have traveled.*
> (Murphy and Brown, 2010)

Today in unfamiliar building complexes we're also worried about retracing our steps back to the parking garage so we can find our cars and head home. The most effective wayfinding programs include Landmarks. Here's a good definition of an effective Landmark:

> *Landmarks that are distinct in shape, color, and appropriately illuminated are memorable, serve to orient people in the space, and provide directional egress information.*
> Patricia Salmi, PhD

Studies in Applied Psychology and in other disciplines have proven that most people use Landmarks every single day to figure out how to get someplace and then return home later.

We might advise a friend coming to visit,

"Turn left at the <u>McDonald's</u>, go two blocks, and then turn right at the <u>first stoplight</u>."

McDonald's and the stoplight are Landmarks – features our brains look for to help us navigate. Inside a building with miles of corridors, we could use three-dimensional architectural features like fountains, archways and sculptures as Landmarks. Or (much less expensively) we can use memorable wall and floor colors and patterns.

Retail Designers already incorporate the concept of Landmarks when they include sparkly attention-grabbing displays or, wall and flooring patterns to attract buyers to the back of stores.

> *That's how good stores operate: You feel almost helplessly pulled in by what you see up ahead, or over there to the right.*
> Paco Underhill, <u>Why We Buy</u>

We can use floor patterns as Landmarks on other project types too.

Design Continuity vs. Memorable, Describable Landmarks

Architects and Interior Designers generally develop a design concept and then apply the imagery consistently everywhere throughout a building complex; corridor intersections, for example. (See Figure 7.6) This works wonderfully in maintaining overall design quality and continuity, and helps promote a strategic branding program.

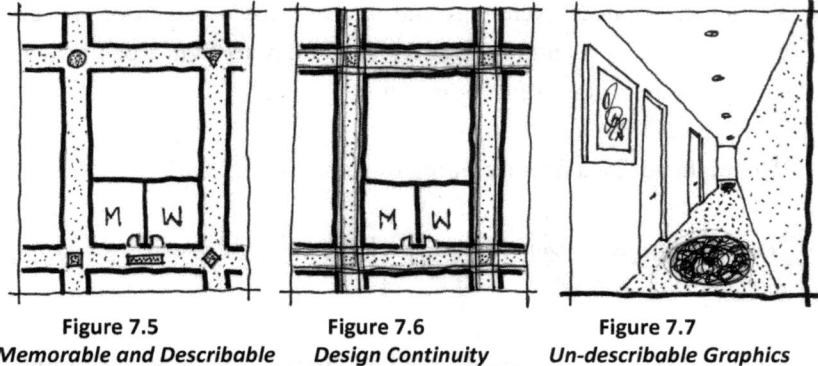

| Figure 7.5 | Figure 7.6 | Figure 7.7 |
| Memorable and Describable | Design Continuity | Un-describable Graphics |

In flooring this design consistency may translate to:
- Large round floral carpet patterns at hotel corridor intersections
- The same geometric flooring shape (in slightly different colors) at entries to Classrooms in an elementary school.
- Matching VCT borders around all the nursing stations on multiple hospital patient floors.
- Identical stone tiles and broadloom carpet on all multi-tenant elevator lobbies in a high-rise building for corporate tenants.

Design continuity may promote design branding and a controlled look throughout a building. But it isn't an effective approach in terms of wayfinding in locations where people need memorably different "knock-em-on-the-head" features (like golden McDonald's arches) to remember where to turn right.

> *In symmetrical environments, wayfinding aids are particularly important (Gulwadi, Joseph, and Keller, 2009). In general, too much symmetry or sameness can make it difficult for visitors to use the environments in which they find themselves and these authors suggest,*
> *"Avoid symmetry. Distinguish areas by using color or materials for easier navigation and wayfinding."*
>   Research Design Connections,
>   https://www.ResearchDesignConnections.com/

Wayfinding studies confirm that Landmarks should be distinct in shape and color, and be "easily describable". (See Figure 7.5)

So forget design subtlety if wayfinding could be a problem for your client.

> *For example, for people with dementia, a model ship... is more effective in wayfinding than a banner, plant or other impersonal cue.*
>   Cynthia Leibrock and Debra Harris, <u>Design Details for Health</u>

It might seem a little kitschy (Okay – it IS kitschy) to most designers, but if a nurse told Ethel from Modesto, *"Turn left at the starfish on the floor, then turn right at the seashell on the floor"*, Ethel would understand that.

"Turn left at the dark grey square" (vs. the "medium grey square" 30 feet earlier) would not have the same memorable impact. Ethel would feel confused and frustrated.

> *Subjects with access to describable landmarks made fewer wayfinding errors, had faster exit completion times, spent less time looking around, re-reading exit route descriptions, and straying from the route than subjects with access to landmarks that were difficult to describe and those who had access to no landmarks.*
>   Informedesign: "Landmarks Improve Wayfinding During Emergencies"

> *Color coding should only use colors that are not confusing to name—yellow and red are easier to name than turquoise (which could be blue or green) or gray (which can take on additional hues, particularly for older eyes).*
>   (Dalke, Little, Niemann, Camgoz, Steadman, Hill, and Stott, 2006)

Vinyl, Rubber and Carpet Seaming Opportunities

New floor seaming technology is fabulous in its ability to create colorful and intricate designs. Applying this technology to create memorable Landmarks at locations where people can become confused about direction can be a valuable component of a successful wayfinding program. But to be most effective, this means we need to avoid designing extremely complex patterns that someone giving instructions can't describe in just a few words. (See Figure 7.7)

Moving from Landmark to Landmark

Studies recommend designing multiple consecutive Landmarks in interiors (so the next floor pattern Landmark, for example, is visible from the last one). When someone can look ahead and know they are still going in the right direction, then they will feel more confident (back to Hansel's idea – a bright boy).

> *Colored surfaces used as landmarks make it easier for us to find our way through a space, even when the colors are simply painted on posts at navigational decision points without any accompanying text.*
> *(Helvacioglu and Olgunturk, 2011)*

For example, the Lobby Receptionist could tell Ethel,
"Keep looking for the butterflies on the floor until you reach the Pharmacy."

And the Middle School Administrator could tell Max,
"Follow the black stars on the floor to the Multi-Purpose Room and Cafeteria"

> *Serving as Landmarks, displays should be planned for every 20 feet: personal cues are 50% more effective than traditional signage.*
> *Cynthia Leibrock and Debra Harris, <u>Design Details for Health</u>*

Studies show that it's easier for most people to remember colors and shapes than cardinal directions. So while the majority of designers may not want butterflies, black stars, or other themed shapes in their corridors, if that makes life less frustrating for Ethel and Max (and can help reduce the need for additional signage) then shouldn't we consider this "Disneyland" strategy in buildings where people frequently get lost?

> *...the environment offers a multitude of cues: the perceiver must make sense of the most important ones to function effectively in a setting...Some people (infants or those cast suddenly into a new setting) may be perceptually confused because they are overwhelmed with cues and have not yet learned to sort the important from the unimportant ones."*
> Egon Brunswick, <u>Environmental Psychology Principles and Practice</u>

Wayfinding Design Action Steps:

1. Develop your overall Schematic Design Ideas including design style, colors, architectural features etc.

2. Look at your floor plan to determine where the majority of people will be heading (and where you will <u>want</u> to lead them). These are the Pathways that your design can instinctively reinforce with floor color and accent features.

3. Locate the places where the largest number of people will need to make a decision about where to go next so you can purposely design easily describable Landmarks with floor patterns.

> *In highly sought-out areas such as elevator banks, Martin suggests introducing additional colors, patterns, and textures to draw visitors there without depending upon signage alone.*
> *"You're not only reading, you're getting the reinforcement of a material and a transition," she says. "If you just see beige floor for miles and miles, it doesn't cue you that something is happening."*
> Barbara Martin, KMA Design, Healthcare Design Online

4. Develop two or three floor pattern alternates for both Pathway and Landmark Design (using some of the strategies described in this chapter) that reinforce your Schematic Design scheme.

Have fun developing wayfinding design ideas!

Traditionally, only Restaurant and Casino Designers could "push a theme" while other design professionals must design with aesthetic continuity, subtlety and restraint.

Forget That!

Use your imagination to develop your theme and decide what colors, shapes and images would create memorable and easily describable flooring Landmarks for your project type.

- If a Senior Housing Facility has a nature-based design theme, then differently colored and types of leaves, flowers or trees could be appropriate.
- At a VA hospital, a floor pattern with differently colored American State shapes at major corridor intersections could be appropriate and memorable.

5. Select the most vulnerable end-user you can imagine for your project type, like Ethel or Max. Then let your avatar "walk the route" as though you are inside the plan (if the project is still in planning stages) or in reality if you are changing the flooring in an existing building. Pretend you are lost and need clear Landmark directions.

The concept of city images helps us understand why most of us see cities in terms of elements such as the Eiffel Tower and London Bridge (which Lynch calls Landmarks).
John Zeisel, Inquiry by Design

6. Evaluate your flooring alternates and then develop your most successful scheme, blending Architectural Design Psychology with your own design ideas.

Let your client know what you are doing!

Your clients will be impressed when you explain that your design concepts can help with their wayfinding problems. Let them know how your floor pattern recommendations will support their operational and business goals.

> *Clients lose faith in the reliability of the architect if they perceive a deficiency of knowledge of business and economics...*
> The Center for Health Design, <u>Evidence Based Design</u>

IN THIS CHAPTER YOU LEARNED THAT FLOOR PATTERNS CAN BE AN IMPORTANT ELEMENT IN ANY WAYFINDING PROGRAM BY:

- CREATING PATHWAYS THAT PEOPLE WILL FOLLOW (BRAINS FOLLOWING FEET)
- CREATING LANDMARKS THAT PEOPLE WILL REMEMBER (FEET FOLLOWING BRAINS)

> *We feel before we think.*
> *Instincts are powerful. They color our every thought and are the root of our actions.*
> "Living Office," by Herman Miller, 2013

> *Within the architectural context, flooring is of fundamental importance in creating a sense of narrative and of depth for the user's experience of space. As the ground on which all other experiences rest, flooring can elevate less noble materials, enhance lackluster design, and help to resolve problems of flow, wayfinding, and proportion.*
> Alex Stark, Feng Shui Consultant

HIDDEN MESSAGE #8:

Yin/Yang is the Goldilocks Principle: Too much? Too little? Or just right...

> Yin and Yang, the two primordial forces that govern the universe, symbolize harmony. They are opposites... but unlike Western ideas of conflicting extremes, yin and yang are complementary. They depend on each other. Without dark there is no light. Without hot, there is no cold... like a magnet's positive and negative poles, yin and yang unite.
> Sarah Rossbach, <u>The Chinese Art of Placement</u>

THIS CHAPTER WILL HELP YOU SELECT FLOOR PATTERNS THAT WILL PROMOTE YOUR CLIENT'S SPECIFIC PERSONAL AND BUSINESS GOALS LIKE PRODUCTIVITY, CREATIVITY AND CONCENTRATION.

YOUR CLIENTS WILL LOVE YOU FOR LISTENING TO THEM WHILE POSITIVELY IMPACTING THEIR "BOTTOM LINE" THROUGH DESIGN.

This is an easy flooring psychology principle to use during all stages of the design process from Site Planning to selecting final interior finishes including flooring, furniture and artwork. During the Programming Phase you can determine if the inhabitants of a specific room, area, department, building or site will psychologically and/or physically benefit from a lower, balanced or higher-energy environment. Then you can design the appropriate spaces by selecting and combining specific features from the Yin/Yang Energy Charts below.

> *Yin and Yang together constitute the Tao – "the Way" – the eternal principle of heavenly and earthly harmony. In Feng Shui, applying the Yin and Yang concept brings about balance and harmony, which in turn brings good fortune.*
> Lillian Too, <u>The Complete Illustrated Guide to Feng Shui</u>

> *All changes, as well as so-called balance or equilibrium, are produced and given life by the intersecting of opposites.*
> Georges Ohsawa, <u>Unique Principle</u>

Yin / Yang Energy Charts

Floor Features

Lower Energy Yin Features	**Higher Energy Yang Features**
Cool Colors	Warm Colors
(Blues, greens, purples)	*(Yellows, oranges, reds)*
Dark and Greyed Tones	Light and Bright Tones
Solid Colored Flooring	Multi-Colored Flooring
Small Patterns	Large Patterns
Curving Patterns	Angled Patterns
Symmetrical/Regular Patterns	Asymmetrical/Irregular
Low Contrast Patterns	High Contrast Patterns
One Texture	Multiple Textures
Monolithic Tile Layout	Quarter-Turn Tile Layout
Rectangular Flooring Layout	Diagonal Flooring Layout
Soft Flooring	Hard Flooring

Other Design Features to Consider

Lower Energy Yin Features	Higher Energy Yang Features
Horizontal Bldg. Shape & Details	Vertical Bldg. Shape & Details
Round, Square, Rectangular Forms	Angled and Pointed Forms
Minimal Landscaping	Lush Green Trees & Plants
Symmetrical / Balanced Layouts	Asymmetrical / Imbalanced
Monochromatic Environment	Hi-Contrast Multi-Colored
Cool Wall, Furniture, Fabric Colors	Warm Wall, Furniture, Fabrics
Low Ceilings	High Ceilings
Low Light Levels	High Light Levels
Small Windows	Large Windows
Minimalist Design Detailing	Ornamental Design Detailing
Naturalistic Landscape Artwork	Abstract Artwork
Soft Classical or Jazz Music	Loud Rock, Hip Hop, Country
Well Organized Places	Cluttered and Chaotic Places
Mood: low, subdued, reflective	Mood: high, bright, lively

If the wall colors, furniture and artwork create a very low-energy space, for example, then your flooring specification can either:

- reinforce that feeling when you recommend low-energy floor colors and patterns.
- create a higher-energy space when you recommend floor colors and patterns that will <u>increase</u> the energy.

The lower the existing energy in a place, the higher the energy your flooring would need to have in order to shift the overall energy. There is only so much one architectural feature can do. But combining high-energy flooring with warm bright accent wall colors, for example, would noticeably increase the energy in any space (and the occupant's energy).

Architectural determinism: Theory that there is a direct relationship between the built environment and a particular behavior.
  Dak Kopec, <u>Environmental Psychology for Design</u>

I. How do you know what energy level is best to meet your client's goals?

During the Programming Phase, you can simply ask your client,

- *"Would your staff (or end-users) be more satisfied and/or productive if they were more motivated and energized?"*
    If so, then your client would benefit from a <u>higher</u>-energy space that would help people increase their personal energy levels.

- *"Would your staff (or end-users) be more satisfied and/or productive if they were less stressed and overwhelmed?"*
    If so, then your client would benefit from a <u>lower</u>-energy space that would help people decrease their personal energy levels.

> *Feng Shui and Sacred Geometry can be used to create harmony, health, and fortune in everyday life. Their goal is to make life easier and more conducive to achievement of personal, communal or institutional potential.*
> *Alex Stark, Feng Shui Consultant, www.AlexStark.com*

However, there is one critical concept that you'll need to remember: Studies show that people typically <u>say</u> that they prefer higher-energy features (like bold colors and abstract art) when they are in a familiar setting (home or workplace) feeling relaxed.

According to studies, those same people will prefer lower-energy features (like calming colors and landscape scenes) in environments they find more stressful. So you will always need to evaluate the programming information you receive from your clients based upon this realization and your project type.

After you receive programming information from your client, you will still need to switch your perspective from "safe healthy designer" to your "vulnerable end-user."

Then you can ask yourself,
"Which energy level will help you (experiencing the space like your vulnerable Avatar) feel most comfortable and confident?

- *When you approach the building - driving or walking?"*
  (to help you determine building exterior materials and details; paving colors and patterns).

- *When you enter and move through the building's public spaces?"*
  (to help you select the best <u>overall</u> interior energy level, and then decide how your flooring materials, colors and patterns will contribute to that energy level target).

- *When you enter different departments, areas and rooms?'*
  (to help shift the energy slightly up or down through a variation of the flooring material, colors and patterns to produce specific preferred behavior in those places).

> *Where there is high brightness (illumination) and warm colors (red, pink, orange, yellow) there is a tendency for human beings to be physically aroused and to direct that attention outward into the environment. Such a combination might be quite suitable for convalescent patient, maternity patients, or anyone on the way to recovery.*
>
> *Where there is less brightness and cooler colors, there is a tendency for human beings to be relaxed. This kind of environment would be good for chronic patients and for those who are likely to be institutionalized for long periods.*
>   Andrew Baum and Jerome Singer, <u>Advances in Environmental Psychology</u>

You can determine energy goals for every project type from residential, healthcare, corporate, retail and hospitality to industrial. This can easily become a standard part of your Programming and Information Gathering process. It's just something that Architects and Interior Designers haven't typically considered important in the past since research hasn't been available to guide us in a specific design direction.

II. A Balanced Energy Level is The Best Default

> *The best and safest thing is to keep a balance in your life, acknowledging the great powers around us and in us. If you can do that, and live that way, you are really a wise man.*
> Euripides (484 BC – 406BC)

Most children know the story about Goldilocks and the Three Bears. Little lost Goldilocks finds herself inside the Bears' house and finds:
Porridge that's not too hot... not too cold... but just right...
A chair that's not too big... not too small... but just right...
A bed that's not too hard... not too soft... but just right...

And bringing the subject back to energy;
Not too yin (low energy)...not too yang (high energy)...
But just right (balanced energy)...

Most people prefer an environment with balanced energy, although some individuals feel most supported in a lower-energy environment (like my friend Megan who lives in a serene and clutter-free beige and light blue house). Others feel most supported in a much higher-energy environment (like my friend Margot who worked for the Peace Corps and surrounds herself with vibrant Caribbean colors and objects).

Achieving a balanced energy level should be the design default if your client's purpose isn't reinforced by either extreme since it helps maintain the health and happiness of the largest number of people. You will be designing "for the greatest good." Service vs. Ego – your choice.

> *To keep the proper relation between Yin and Yang, it is necessary to maintain a balance between the two. If a "deficiency" or "predominance" of any force of Yin or Yang occurs, the balance is disturbed and so happiness, health or fortune will be disturbed.*
> Roger Green, Feng Shui Consultant

Finding the right balance between solitude and interaction is a key problem in today's work environments. Too little interaction leads to isolation and stagnation. Too much leads to distractions and stress. Somewhere in between is the "happiness zone" where challenge, creativity, and innovation are most likely to occur. Understanding how this zone shifts for tasks, individuals, and the deep structure of work is a major challenge for designers.

  Judith Heerwagen, <u>Biophilic Design</u>

Equalizing or balancing opposite qualities is the simplest way to bring your space into harmony with nature. Just remember that too much of anything diminishes everything else.

  Angel Thompson, <u>Feng Shui: How to Achieve the Most Harmonious Arrangement of your Home or Office</u>

Johnson's Baby Center needed a <u>high-energy</u> floor for a <u>low-energy</u> office space to create a <u>balanced-energy</u> workplace.

One day a Carpet Dealer I've worked with many times called me in desperation (really – <u>desperation</u>). A flood had destroyed his long-term client's first floor carpet and they had decided to replace all the carpet on both of their two large floors.

He was completely frustrated because he had already shown his clients about fifty carpet tile samples from a variety of manufacturers. The office directors had criticized EVERYTHING. He didn't know what direction to take next since they had conflicting opinions about which carpet colors and patterns would be best.

I said I would help. I knew that these clients needed to be led into understanding that there <u>was</u> a best direction after floundering for so long. A subjective design discussion with my saying,

"I recommend <u>this</u> color and pattern more than <u>that</u> color and pattern" would never lead to a decision.

So I arrived 30 minutes ahead of time to walk through and experience the design energy in the space on my own, hoping that would lead me in a particular design direction that would seem logical to the directors.

(I'm presently writing a <u>Fast-Action Flooring Psychology Guide</u> that will be available in Summer 2015 to help you evaluate a place's existing design energy quickly so you can more easily – and logically - develop color and pattern recommendations when your client exclusively requests new flooring.)

My question to myself, "How does this space make me FEEL?"
My immediate answer: "It makes me feel drab with VERY low energy. The grey feels deadening."

The Johnson's Baby Center is in an older building in downtown San Francisco. The building is very interesting with unusual architectural features like natural wood columns and beams. The Second Floor overlooks the First Floor Reception Area. Both floors have low ceilings and large Open Office areas filled with grey workstations (grey fabric panels, grey plastic laminate counters and grey files). Except for black, grey is the lowest-energy color, so the low dark wood ceilings combined with the grey furniture to make this a very low-energy Yin space.

The directors obviously felt the same way since they had painted all the wood office doors a variety of different almost-neon colors. This color palette isn't at all standard in corporate office design - just pre-school projects, in my experience - although this direction was in keeping with the staff's mission to market and sell Baby Products. The bright door colors provided energy blasts at the perimeter, but couldn't counteract the tired feeling inside the huge Open Office areas.

I knew that in order to balance the low ceilings and grey low-energy workstations their new carpet (the only planned renovation) needed to add <u>extremely</u> high energy. Higher energy than I had ever previously proposed on a project.

FLOORING PSYCH • 143

First I talked to the directors about how their architecture, finishes and furniture combined to create a very low-energy work environment. Then I suggested that their new carpet could help raise the energy in the space. This would result in making their staff more enthusiastic, energetic and productive.

The directors agreed with my "high-energy carpet" approach. It wasn't difficult convincing them since they hadn't had a verbalized research-based design approach up to that point and were very frustrated themselves just talking subjectively about which carpet design would be best.

So... thinking about Yin and Yang energy, I knew that:

- One carpet tile style, however boldly colored or patterned would still not raise the energy level high enough.

- A rectilinear layout would not add enough energy.

The highest energy carpet I could imagine was a very bright, multi-colored, irregular, asymmetrical and diagonal pattern.
(See Figures 8.1, 8.2 and 8.3)

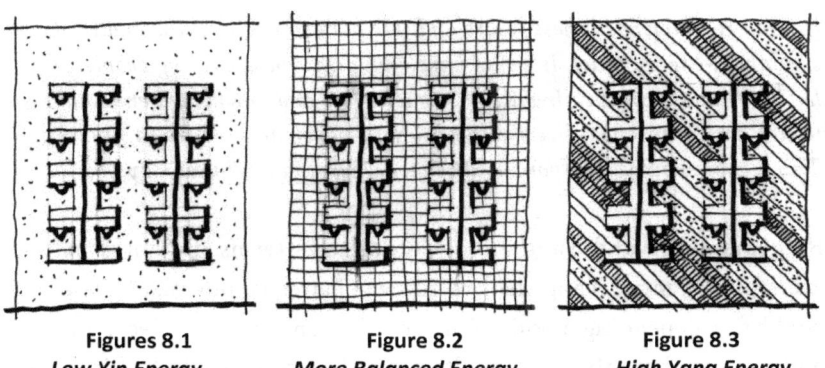

| Figures 8.1 | Figure 8.2 | Figure 8.3 |
| Low Yin Energy | More Balanced Energy | High Yang Energy |

The Effect of Floor Pattern Energy below Workstations

My final recommendations and carpet samples were immediately approved.

We would:
- Select five solid-colored carpet tiles (all really bright colors that would pop: yellow, green, blue, purple, and red) from the same carpet collection; they looked great together.
- Install these colored tiles in a wall-to-wall striped pattern.
- Vary the colored stripe widths from 1 to 4 tiles wide.
- Extend the stripes diagonally across each floor underneath all the grey cubes to give each workstation at least two bright colors to counteract the grey stations.

MAXIMUM ENERGY!

End Result:
After installation, the new carpet totally changed the look and feel of the Baby Center. The environment shifted from low to balanced energy that is in sync with their goal of attracting and keeping young dynamic staff members. The clients and my carpet dealer friend were very happy. Having a practical business-related reason to select one carpet over another made sense to them.

Cautionary note:
If I had recommended these colors and this pattern to a client who already had a balanced-energy space, it would have been disastrous! Pushing people's energy too high creates conflict, inability to concentrate and heightened emotions. That would have translated directly into staff turnover and decreased productivity. Think about how you respond and behave when <u>you</u> are in sensory-overload!

Remember Yin and Yang are always relative terms. Diagonal patterns are typically more Yang than rectilinear patterns, but that relationship could flip depending upon color, contrast and pattern. See Figure 8.4 and evaluate how the Yang multi-colored pattern would feel in a rectilinear layout compared to the Yin single color pattern laid diagonally.

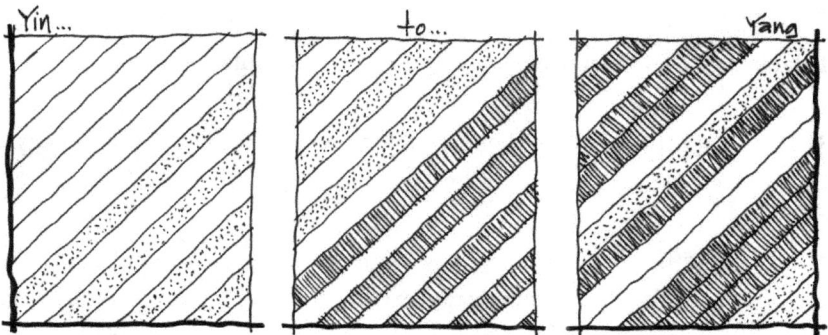

Figure 8.4
Diagonal Stripes with Increasing Energy from left to right, Yin to Yang

Look at the Yin/Yang Features Chart for a generalized approach but then use your imagination and the Squint Test to carry this concept further to meet your own design goals and your client's purpose.

> Life is a condition alternating between excitation, destruction, and unbalance - and reorganization, equilibrium and rest. In the course of life colors play their role. Each color has a special importance and all colors together help to guarantee normal life.
> Kurt Goldstein, Psycho-neurologist, <u>The Organism</u>

III. Beyond Balance: Using Higher and Lower Energy Levels can help you "Design with a Purpose"

Balanced energy design schemes are typically best for a group of people (whether family members or staff sharing a work environment) but there are exceptions depending upon the tasks to be done in a space.

> You need to consider what people will be doing in any space you're designing. A space for working on a routine task should be different from a space for brainstorming, and a space for socializing should be different than a space for meditating.
> Sally Augustin PhD,
> <u>Place Advantage: Applied Psychology for Interior Architecture</u>

There are two main reasons why you would not choose to default to balanced-energy design schemes for groups of people:

- Slightly imbalanced energy might be best if the majority needs a major energy shift (up or down) for a specific reason.

- Slightly imbalanced energy might be best in a home if everyone is healthy psychologically except for <u>one</u> family member, in which case the best energy level might be the one that helps the weakest person.

IV. When is a Lower-Energy Environment Best?

> *Another research team concludes that... fewer stimuli (e.g., cooler or darker colors, artwork depicting nature scenes) for those setting in which creative or high-demand tasks are performed.*
> Dak Kopec, <u>Environmental Psychology for Design</u>

Low Energy at Home:

Slightly lower-energy environments are best if these are the things you or your clients want to do when you come home:
- *Relax and wind down after a difficult day.*
- *Enjoy a good thoughtful conversation with friends or family.*
- *Read, write, study or develop a creative project.*

If these are your goals, then look at the "Lower Energy Yin Features List" for ideas. For example, you could add some cool colors (blues, greens or purples) and task lighting (instead of using bright overhead fixtures) to the room where you'll spend most of your time.

> *Research suggests that reading conducted in blue or pale green environments will yield greater comprehension and retention than in red environments.*
> Dak Kopec, <u>Environmental Psychology for Design</u>

Television programs like "Sell This House" and "Get it Sold" are all about energy level although the word "energy" is never mentioned (let alone chi, prana or ungud). Real Estate Agents on these shows speak in terms of *"what the typical buyer wants."*

Their designers understand that home-buyers are most attracted to a master bedroom that looks like a hotel room at a resort, for example: uncluttered, minimal furniture, soft neutral wall colors with pale blue, teal or green accent colors, low light, lots of fluffy pillows, white towels and candle-light (all features that decrease energy). When bedrooms include these features, then potential buyers can easily imagine themselves falling onto the beds and relaxing. That's the feeling they want to have.

> *Blue stimulation increased their sense of relaxation and lessened their anxiety and hostility.*
> *(Robert Gerard (1958), Dr. Harry Wohlfarth (1958), B. Aaronson (1971) and J.J Plack and J. Schick (1974)*

Low Energy at Work:

Researchers agree that lower energy levels can help workers perform specific tasks better – with the emphasis on the word <u>specific</u>. When you think about some of the following work descriptions and the environments we identify with them, then you'll realize that we already design some spaces to promote energy goals (whether or not we consciously verbalize it that way professionally).

Lowest Energy: Science or Medical Laboratories

The work environments with the lowest energy are generally designed with white, grey and metal finishes. These colors and materials greatly reduce environmental distractions – necessary since intense focus and concentration is needed to quantify exact scientific measurements and results, contain viruses and contaminants etc.

Slightly Lower Energy: Workplaces for Creative People including Designers, Writers and Artists

Creative tasks don't require as much focus as the NHI Researchers in Hazmat suits trying to find a cure for the Zombie plague – but creativity requires a calm environment in order to maximize the brain power that contributes to innovation and original expression. When we think about places where creativity flourishes, stereotypes would be an open studio space with wood floors and tall windows, or a library with a wood desk and bookshelves; both with views of green landscaping.

> *A team led by Lichtenfeld has linked seeing the color green and creative performance. In a rigorous set of experiments that eliminated saturation and brightness as potential explanations... this team "demonstrated that a brief glimpse of green prior to a creativity task enhances creative performance..."*
>   Stephanie Lichtenfeld, Andrew J. Elliot, Markus A. Maier, and Reinhard Pekrun. "Fertile Green: Green Facilitates Creative Performance."
> *Personality and Social Psychology Bulletin*

> *Where professionals are working, using relatively calming colors in spaces where people will be doing more strenuous cognitive tasks... is important.*
> *Green is generally a good color choice in spaces where people are doing work that requires focus and where creative thought is desired.*
> *Red should be avoided in areas where analytical tasks will be performed.*
>   Research Design Connections, 2013 Issue 3

Researchers agree that more challenging tasks should be done in calmer spaces and less challenging tasks should be done in more stimulating spaces.

Think about what you consciously (and unconsciously) do when you perform various tasks. When I need to think creatively to write or design I clean my desk first, listen to the Norah Jones or Andrea Boccelli stations on Pandora, limit distractions (phone on "silent" and no e-mail-checking) and I try to shut out the world. I create a low-energy environment. I bet you do something similar.

Wild Planet Toys needed a low-energy floor to balance the high energy of millions of furniture and toy parts

About ten years ago Wild Planet Toys hired me to provide Architectural and Interior Design Services for their new office in San Francisco. We found a great space that had initially been built out for a dot-com firm. The office came complete with very expensive hi-tech custom Knoll workstations (movable white and gray laminate counters and storage units that fit like jig-saw puzzle pieces around patterned-glass-and-metal-spines with polished metal connectors and hundreds of exposed data cables) - lots and lots of parts and pieces.

The interior design would have been fine for a new tenant that just planned to add a computer to each desk (like the original dot.com firm had intended). But I knew that wouldn't be the case once the creative toy designers at Wild Planet Toys moved into the space!

The existing Wild Planet Toys Office in San Francisco was filled with toys in all stages of development and packaging - clutter on steroids. Every surface (including floors and walls) was covered with toy parts. De-cluttering and tossing would be a gigantic effort prior to the move, and the firm directors anticipated that their new office space would start filling up with new toy pieces and parts as soon as they unpacked boxes.

Clutter and complexity increases energy. But it's not good high energy. It's confused energy and makes us feel like we're not in control.

If you've ever watched an episode of "Hoarders" on television then you know that excessive clutter is overwhelming and isn't psychologically healthy. It makes us feel (consciously and unconsciously) that there is always something that we should be cleaning up, organizing, dumping or doing. It's typically more difficult for people to concentrate and be productive in cluttered environments.

> *An orderly and harmonious space leads to an orderly and harmonious inner life, which is so necessary for the good health of the body, mind and soul – and by extension, of everything that exists around us.*
> Kathleen Cox, <u>Vastu Living</u>

Additionally, the existing carpet in all the corridors, private offices, public spaces and conference rooms had a black, grey and white-striped pattern that added more energy and complexity. Luckily, the workstations sat on charcoal rubber flooring with small grey speckles (low energy).

Wild Planet Toys wanted to keep the barely used custom furniture for their 60 employees, but they agreed to change the striped carpet and a few wall colors to create a more balanced looking and feeling space.

My Recommendations:

- Paint the huge white freestanding columns with deep rich colors to attract attention away from all the tiny colored toy parts.
- Replace the striped carpet with a very dark purple broadloom carpet, a rich but lower energy color (broadloom instead of tile since they didn't need any more pieces).
- Select a curvilinear textured carpet (purple-on-purple circles) to balance the sharp metal angles and points. (See Figure 8.5)

> *In general, objects and patterns with curved features are preferred to those with pointed features and sharp angles. Research has shown that we associate circles with softness, happiness, goodness, love, life, brightness, lightness, warmth, quickness and quietness.*
> Sally Augustin PhD,
> <u>Place Advantage: Applied Psychology for Interior Architecture</u>

My client totally understood the Yin/Yang design approach and why the new purple curvilinear carpet was necessary to help create a more balanced environment. Wild Planet Toys is still in the same space years later, and I've been hired to help with two office expansions – so I know that this research and energy-based approach works for them.

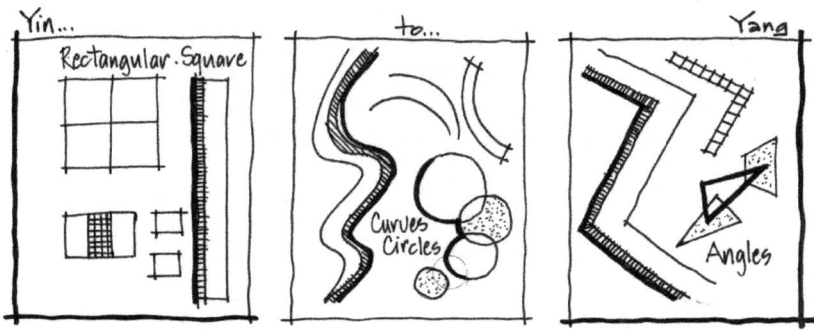

Figure 8.5
Add Curves and Circles to Balance Angles and Points

V. When is a Higher Energy Environment Best?

Higher Energy at Home:
Slightly higher-energy environments are best if you or your clients feel listless and lethargic (for whatever reason) and want to be more productive and purposeful. If these are your goals, then look at the "Higher Energy Yang Features List" for ideas. For example, you could add warmer colors, larger patterns and higher-contrasting fabrics and flooring in the rooms where you'll spend most of your time.

Higher Energy at Work:
Researchers have found that performing routine tasks like filing or data entry is easier in high-energy environments (those with Yang features). On the days that I spend writing invoices, organizing tax information, or performing other tasks that require more discipline than imagination – off goes mild Norah Jones! Those are the times when I work best (and longer) with a "Vikings" or "Game of Thrones" Marathon happening in the background!

> When performing low demand tasks, performance appears to worsen over time in a blue rather than the red environment. Working at a boring task in a calming [blue] environment seems to reduce performance levels, as employees seem to be below an optimal stimulation level. Performing a boring task in a red environment optimizes performance because the stimulation from the environment counters the boring nature of the task.
> Research Design Connections, 2013 Issue 3,
> https://www.ResearchDesignConnections.com/

> Another research team concludes that... more stimuli (e.g., brighter or warmer colors, increased visual and aural stimuli) should be incorporated into work spaces in which routine or low-demand tasks are performed...
> Dak Kopec, *Environmental Psychology for Design*

Higher Energy at Play:

Casino Designers purposely create high-energy environments that promote activity regardless of the time of day or night. Mexican restaurants make great party places because they put everyone in an exuberant Cinco de Mayo mood with plenty of reds, oranges and yellows; bright lighting; loud music; and swaying piñatas (all Yang energy features).

Casino and restaurant designers have been designing with a purpose for decades and are way ahead of most design professionals in identifying the importance of incorporating psychological research in the design process.

> Empirical Studies found that specific colors affect mood, breathing, pulse rate, and blood pressure: Red, orange and yellow light increases the viewer's blood pressure, arousal via palmar conductance, respiratory movements, and eye-blink frequency.
> (Robert Gerard (1958), Dr. Harry Wohlfarth (1958), B. S. Aaronson (1971) and J. J. Plack and J. Schick (1974)

VI. What energy features and strategies can you use to select flooring that helps create lower or higher energy levels?

COLOR:
Cool-Colored Yin Flooring (blues, greens and purples) vs. Warm-Colored Yang Flooring (yellows, oranges and reds)

While reading the following color studies, remember that any feature described as "comfortable, appealing or preferable" reduces energy and stress (which may or may not be your purpose).

> *Color's profound effect on life was probably first recognized by humans when we realized that our existence was dictated by two factors beyond our control: day and night, or light and darkness. All living things are vitalized by the bright reds, oranges, and yellows of daytime, and calmed and rejuvenated by the blues, indigos, and violets of nighttime...*
> *The well-known Greek philosopher Pythagoras (whose theorems served as the basis for architecture) used color therapy 500 years before the birth of Christ.*
>   Jacob Liberman, <u>Light: Medicine of the Future</u>

> *Some things can be said about color in the psychobiological interpretation. For example, blues and greens are generally regarded as restful (in our early experiences in the savannas of Africa these colors stood for shelter, water, and vegetable food sources...)*
>   Grant Hildebrand, University of Washington

> *The stimulation of red and other warm colors tends to increase blood pressure, pulse and respiration. There is greater skin response (palmar conductance) and brain activity. Attention is directed outward toward the environment.*
>   Faber Birren, <u>Color & Human Response</u>

> *The morning star is like a man; he is painted red all over; that is the color of life.*
> Pawnee Chief

Some cautionary concepts to remember about Cool Colors:

Appetite:

The color blue decreases appetite along with energy, according to studies. So don't specify blue or grey as the dominant color in a restaurant or in a dining room if your client wants residents in his Alzheimer's facility to eat more to stay healthy. Painting your kitchen blue or grey might not be a bad idea if you live alone and want to lose those last 10 pounds. A blue bulb inside your refrigerator will make food look less appetizing (by looking slightly moldy).

> *A study in Biological Psychiatry finds that depressed individuals actually do perceive the world as more gray… and the more severe the depression, the more impaired the perception.*
> Psychology Today, December 2010

Age:

Consider the fact that 85% of older people experience yellow tinting of the eye. Think about what happens if you take a clear yellow acetate film and put it over something blue or green. The yellow film makes the blue or green object appear grey and muddy. Positioning the same clear yellow film over a yellow, orange or red object would make those warm colors appear even more intense.

> *Clear color, devoid of gray and black, is most easily seen (by the elderly). Maintain midrange values. Some older people have more difficulty discriminating between cool colors, like blue, green and violet than between warmer tones, like orange and yellow.*
> Victor Regnier, <u>Design for Assisted Living: Guidelines for Housing the Physically and Mentally Frail</u>

SOLIDS AND PATTERNS (SMALL AND LARGE)

Scientists believe that people from all cultures still unconsciously remember the dangers related to the patterns our ancestors viewed on the African savannah. We respond instinctively to similar ground and flooring patterns in our 21st-century environments (indoors and outdoors).

> *The larger the scale of the design, the smaller the group of people the pattern appeals to... There may be evolutionary biological explanations, or lifestyle/behavioral factors at work. A fatigued individual probably is less likely to select a 'busy' combination of florals. Perhaps in our distant past, busy florals in a setting of heavy vegetation concealed danger.*
> Research Design Connections, 2013 Issue 1 (1999)

Savannah Pattern Guidelines:

Viewing patterns increases our energy more than viewing solids.

A green lawn appears more uniform (solid) and lets us see that nothing predatory is coming. Rodents and small animals could approach us beneath taller groundcover and plants (a pattern), so when we view patterns, we pay more attention. This increases our energy more than viewing solid materials and surfaces.

> *More complex or incongruous visual patterns increase the energy levels of viewers.*
> (Mahnke, 1996)

When you evaluate flooring alternates, you could also ask yourself what ground features in nature Conan or Ayla (and your own ancestors) would have found most comfortable to navigate.

- Would a specific floor pattern have looked easy to walk across (like a pebble path?)

- Or difficult (like large stones across a river?)
- Would a pattern look clear and open (like a field of low daisies?)
- Or less certain and safe (like a field of dense high sunflowers?)

Viewing large patterns increases our energy more than viewing small patterns.

> *Where disorientation is a problem in Subacute Care Facilities, orientation can be improved or reduced by pattern. Eliminate bold patterns, stripes, and undulating patterns...*
> *Avoid high-contrast patterns in floor coverings, which can make small objects on the surface difficult to locate... for people with low vision.*
> Cynthia Leibrock and Debra Harris, <u>Design Details for Health</u>

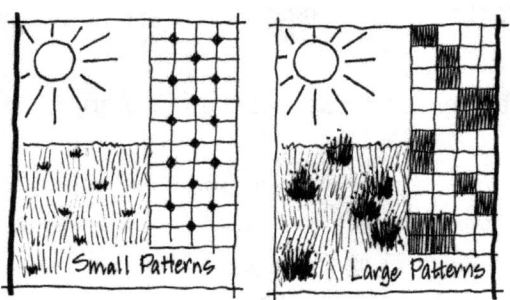

Figure 8.6   Figure 8.7
Pattern Size Influences Energy and Stress
(Is something hiding behind that bush?)

Large animals and predators moving through the grasses create BIG patterns. Tiny harmless creatures moving through the grasses create SMALL patterns. Close shades of gold and green (a small pattern) could just indicate a variation in the grass, not different objects.

Look at your floor pattern from a distance: *Is it a hedgehog - or a lion?* (See Figures 8.6 and 8.7)

FLOORING PSYCH • 157

Limiting textures and colors in interior décor is helpful for the many people with mental illness who are susceptible to sensory overload. Low intensity colors, especially for background surfaces, are most appropriate for this population.
Cynthia Leibrock and Debra Harris, <u>Design Details for Health</u>

Viewing vertical stripes increases our energy more than viewing horizontal stripes.

In nature, when the horizon line on a grassy plain or over water is flat (a horizontal line), then the wind is slow and the waves are low. The world is a safer place and our human energy and stress levels decrease too. In our built-environments, horizontal lines and stripes (or in the case of flooring, stripes perpendicular to our path) also feel more stable and decrease our energy and anxiety. (See Figure 8.8)

Figure 8.8   Figure 8.9
Stripes have the Same Energy as Horizontal and Vertical Features in Nature

In nature, when we view vertical elements like high waves, tall trees and mountains, then our human energy increases to meet the challenges. Patterns designed with vertical stripes (or in the case of flooring, stripes leading straight ahead and parallel to our path) can also intentionally or unintentionally increase our energy and anxiety. (See Figure 8.9)

What type of stripe you decide to incorporate should depend upon the energy of the other design features in the space and your client's goals.

Other factors can also increase or decrease the energy in a pattern.

Whether a pattern appears small or large, Yin or Yang, isn't just based upon the specific carpet, tile, stone, linoleum, or wood style and color. Joint or grout thickness and color contrast contribute to the overall pattern too. Tile direction also plays a large role – its importance depending upon the tile style.
(See Figure 8.10)

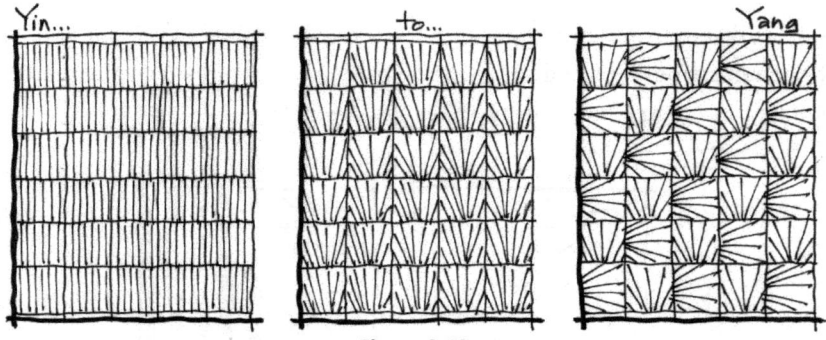

Figure 8.10
Increasing Energy by Accenting Joints and Changing Tile Direction

Room scale should also be considered. We typically feel more comfortable when large patterns are located in large open spaces (not corridors or small rooms). Then people can see the "big picture" and understand the overall design since the pattern isn't disappearing under furniture or around corners. Large patterns that are out of scale with rooms become abstract. Research has proven that people unconsciously try to understand abstract patterns. When they can't understand what the artist or designer intended, then their stress increases.

> A study in a Swedish hospital found that heart-surgery patients in ICU's who were assigned an abstract picture had worsened health outcomes compared to a control group assigned no pictures.
> "A Review of the Research Literature on Evidence-Based Healthcare Design" HERD, Spring 2008

> *Autobiographies of patients who at one time were upset or delirious mention that they perceived ambiguous patterns as frightening demons and other items consistent with their delusions.*
>
> "Floor Designs Can Be Therapeutic", Robert Sommer

Furniture is so important that flooring decisions should not be made looking at a floor pattern in an empty room (or on a plan) unless the room will stay empty. To understand how a space will be experienced by end-users, we need to view furniture and flooring simultaneously.

A pattern will seem large or small depending upon contrast. Herringbone and checkerboard patterns, for example, can create higher or lower energy depending upon color variation and contrast.

> *Although older people require more contrast between colors, it is important that designers avoid creating too much contrast (i.e., black and white, black and yellow, and so on), particularly within patterns, which could lead to a three-dimensional illusion.*
>
> Dak Kopec, Environmental Psychology for Design

Remember that even though I keep connecting increasing energy with higher stress, that relationship isn't always negative - depending upon your client's goals!

Increasing energy and stress with a large striped flooring design was a good thing at the overly grey and dark Johnson's Baby Center. Combining high-energy flooring with the low-energy environment produced a balanced overall energy.

You will need to decide when increasing energy with floor patterns would be a good thing for your client (or not) depending upon the energy in wall, ceiling and door finishes, lighting, furniture and fabrics (and whatever else will be affecting the overall energy in the spaces you design). Flooring selection is just part of the larger energy puzzle.

SYMMETRY AND CONTRAST
Symmetrical/Regular Yin Patterns vs. Asymmetrical/Irregular Yang Patterns

The human mind is constantly drawn to anything that embodies some aspect of symmetry. Our brain seems programmed to notice and search for order and structure.
  Marcus Du Sautoy, <u>Symmetry: A Journey into the Patterns of Nature</u>

Visually appealing images also are symmetrical – and that symmetry can be radial or bilateral... we feel so positively toward things that are symmetrical because most animals have radial or bilateral symmetry and "there is a high premium on being able to detect living things. So it serves as an early-alert system."
  Vilayanur Ramachandran and Elizabeth Seckel,
  "Neurology of Visual Aesthetics", 2014

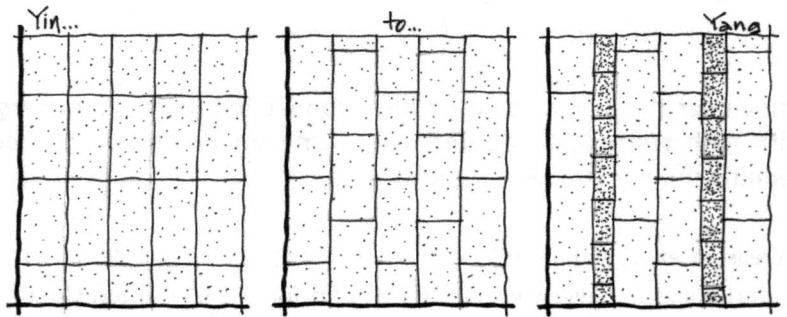

Figure 8.11
Increasing Energy with Irregularity, Asymmetry and Contrast

Human beings connect physiologically and psychologically to structures embodying organized (regular) complexity more strongly than to environments that are either too plain or present disorganized (irregular) complexity.
  (Salingaros 2006)

Mixing Yin / Yang Energy: A Law Firm Story

One of my clients is a law firm specializing in Wills, Trusts, and Estate Planning. Their office felt very hushed and low energy to me when I first stepped into their Reception Area and viewed their Open Office Area. I imagined that they could have issues with staff productivity and motivation. Before even meeting the partners, I thought that if they renewed their lease, I would recommend replacing their tired solid blue broadloom carpet with a warmer colored larger-patterned carpet.

During Programming, I asked the partners whether they thought their staff could benefit from more motivation (a balanced or higher-energy design approach) or decreased stress (a lower-energy design approach). They responded that that the staff energy in the Open Office Areas did seem a little low. But they surprised me by saying that they liked that same low-energy feeling in the Private Offices and Conference Rooms where they met with their clients. In those rooms, emotions could run high, since their clients were often upset discussing the intimate and dysfunctional details of their family lives while planning for their own deaths (not a surprise once I thought about it).

Additionally, the law firm planned to sublease some offices and a small workstation area to attorneys who specialized in Litigation. I asked what it felt like visiting the office of the litigating attorneys. My clients said that people "always seemed to be yelling."

So instead of creating an overall balanced-energy design (as I first anticipated) these became my energy design goals during Programming:

- Create <u>very low energy</u> in the subleased spaces for the litigators (to limit the yelling).
- Create <u>slightly low energy</u> in the estate planning attorney Offices and Conference Rooms (to keep client emotions under control)

- Create <u>balanced energy</u> in the Open Offices, Reception and Staff Areas since the number of staff members and the variety in their work tasks meant that some people would personally benefit from slightly higher energy and some would personally benefit from slightly lower energy.

Considering that this was an 8,500-square-foot space, it didn't make financial or design sense to change typical wall colors and flooring to meet the three different energy levels (although that may have been a good choice in a much larger facility with separate departments). I recommended a balanced-energy carpet (warm colors, low contrast and mid-size pattern).

Note: Balanced energy can be achieved by mixing color, contrast, pattern size, tile orientation etc. in a <u>wide</u> variety of ways. Just be aware that if you pick higher energy in some categories (like color and pattern size) then you need to select lower energy features in other categories (like contrast and tile layout).

Although the architectural envelope would be standard throughout the Law Office, we could change accent wall colors (one wall per room) and artwork content and color to increase or decrease the energy levels in specific rooms to meet their goals. (i.e., no bright warm-colored accent walls, high-contrast fabrics, or abstract red-colored artwork for those loud litigators!)

Mixing Yin / Yang Energy: A Family Story

We notice when a home is designed with an imbalanced energy approach (like an all-white minimalist house in Architect magazine – or a Miami apartment with exuberant Caribbean colors and artwork in Interior Design magazine). An imbalanced environment is totally fine with just one or two occupants who feel supported and nurtured by that imbalance. But with a larger family, there may be someone who feels out of sync and unsupported in his or her own home.

Family Energy Example:

Lethargic slightly depressed 10-year-old Ben is doing badly in school and comes home to a low-energy house. The all-beige walls, cream leather furniture and light maple wood flooring help his hyper-active high-school-teaching, and basketball-coaching father, and his retail-store-owning mother wind down at the end of their overwhelmingly hectic days. But the low energy design scheme is not helping unmotivated Ben.

In this case, it would be good to maintain lower Yin features in the parents' private spaces (their bedroom, living room and home office) and introduce higher Yang features in the rooms where Ben spends his time (Ben's bedroom and the family room).

- In Ben's bedroom: Add a high-contrast area rug, warm paint color, bright sheets and a patterned comforter (Batman? Solar System? Stripes?) Ben should choose colors and patterns.

- In the family room: Since the family is purchasing new flooring, selecting a rich-colored or highly figured hardwood or laminate plank flooring, a warm-colored area rug and bright high-contrast pillows and artwork would increase the room's (and Ben's) energy.

What about Ben's older sister, Sophie? Sophie is in high school, in-and-out of the house, and doing well academically and socially. Sophie's bedroom can reflect her personal energy needs and she will be just fine.

Note: When I first began studying Asian Compass School Feng Shui, I learned that the birth date of the Father should determine the orientation of key features in the home and its energy level. That seemed like a very chauvinistic concept. Then one of my teachers pointed out that throughout history the Father has historically been the main breadwinner in a family. Since the family fortune (and food supply) rose or fell depending upon the success of the Father, it benefitted all family members if the Father prospered.

One of my Feng Shui teachers said that, in families where survival and food supply is no longer an issue, creating an energetic environment that supports the weakest family member is often the best and kindest approach.

As a default, a mixture of energy levels throughout the house will benefit the physical and psychological health of the entire family. People can seek out a place where the energy level will help them most at a given moment in time.

> *This seductive home courts you with an array of different spaces – big and small, open and sheltered, extroverted and introverted – that you can choose from, depending on how you're feeling at the time.*
> Winifred Gallagher, <u>House Thinking</u>

IN THIS CHAPTER YOU LEARNED:

- THE IMPORTANCE OF ADDING QUESTIONS ABOUT OPTIMAL ENERGY LEVEL TO THE INFORMATION GATHERING PROGRAMMING PHASE FOR THE ENTIRE PROPERTY, THE BUILDING, AREAS, DEPARTMENTS AND ROOMS.

- HOW TO INCREASE AND DECREASE ENERGY BY COMBINING YIN AND YANG FLOORING AND OTHER DESIGN FEATURES TO PROMOTE YOUR CLIENT'S SPECIFIC GOALS.

In order for the light to shine so bright, the darkness must be present.
Francis Bacon (1561 – 1626)

HIDDEN MESSAGE #9:

People need Natural Habitats too

You and I are molded by the land, the trees, the sky, and all that surrounds us.
    Bernard Maybeck

IN THIS CHAPTER YOU WILL LEARN HOW TO IDENTIFY NATURE-BASED FLOOR PATTERNS THAT WILL IMPROVE COMFORT AND HEALTH – AND THOSE THAT WON'T.

For human survival and mental health and fulfillment, we need the natural setting in which the human mind almost certainly evolved and in which culture has developed over these millions of years of evolution.
    E.O Wilson, E.O. "Arousing Biophilia"

I. STORY OF THE FROG IN THE LABORATORY

Pretend that, 20 years ago, your grandfather (a renowned scientist in Alaska) moved two frogs from a Louisiana marsh into his Fairbanks laboratory to keep him company. You've inherited his lab and notice that the frogs' descendants are looking a little puny, wobbly and sad. They are not hopping around much and are no longer croaking enthusiastically. You (a renowned scientist yourself) decide to move to Alaska, renovate the lab, and help the frogs at the same time.

Design Approach A:
- Do you decide that the frogs may need a new larger metal cage?
- With your favorite colorful Jackson Pollock print on the wall?
- And would you decide to paint the walls a cheerful bright yellow and install the latest award-winning grey Italian porcelain plank floor tile?

Will those changes help the frogs?

Or...

Design Approach B:
- Do you design an environment that looks as much as possible like the Louisiana marsh where their ancestors hopped happily?
- And paint the ceiling blue with faux-white clouds instead of installing new white acoustic tiles with 2x4 parabolic fixtures?
- And construct a dirt-bottomed pond with green plants?
- And program the lights for daytime and nighttime cycles?
- And increase the temperature and humidity?
- And play a CD of swamp sounds?
- And do whatever else you imagine will look, feel and sound like "home" to Louisiana frogs?

Or...

Design Approach C:
- Do you wait for quantifiable scientific frog studies (like the Evidence Based Design Studies being conducted today to decide what hospitals should look like) before you make any changes?
- Do you delay programming your lights until a highly qualified researcher conducts multiple controlled studies comparing frog health under 24 hour lighting vs. day/night lighting cycles?
- Do you delay making any changes for a few years until peer-reviewed studies evaluate your <u>exact</u> frog species' preferences?

ARE YOU EVEN CONSIDERING DESIGN APPROACHES 'A' AND 'C'? OF COURSE NOT!

You (being a sensitive designer as well as scientist) would probably try to make the place look, sound and feel as much like a natural marsh as possible and then fine-tune it as you (and the frogs) go along. That's the design approach zoo designers would take after doing research into a specific species' natural habitat. But that's not the approach most designers take when we create spaces for our clients. Studies in Environmental Psychology confirm that we believe people aren't as dependent upon their environments (or nature) as are the other creatures on our planet.

> *Interactional Theory... declares that people and the environment are separate entities that constantly interact.*
> *Transactional Theory... contends that the human-environment relationship is mutually supportive.*
>
> *Ironically, humans seem to have little difficulty understanding the transactional relationship between the environment and other life forms, but when it comes to their own species, most cling to an interactional perspective.*
>   Dak Kopec, <u>Environmental Psychology for Design</u>

Our belief that we don't need the natural world as much as animals do is a relatively new belief. The advent of Judeo-Christian culture about 2,500 years ago took humans <u>out</u> of the universally-accepted Circle of Life and convinced us that, *"Man is made in the image and likeness of God."* That gave us permission to feel superior to earth's other creatures and use the Earth for our own purposes (responsible or irresponsible).

Since most of the world's population (in every country) lived and worked on farms just 100 years ago, people still retained a strong connection with nature. The majority of people have only clustered in cities and lived in artificial environments for the past 50 years (a blip in time) – which WE often design based upon the design trend of the decade.

Isn't it just common sense that people need nurturing natural habitats too? No reputable zoologist would put an ape in an 8' x 10' white room with fluorescent light for 8 hours a day, far from a window, force him to stay awake hours after the sun has set, and expect him to thrive.

> *When a man does not realize his kinship with the world, he lives in a prison whose walls are alien to him. When he meets the eternal spirit in all objects... then he finds himself in perfect truth, and his harmony with the all is established.*
>   Rabindranath Tagore, <u>Sadhana</u>

Even in the oldest Zoos, there is generally a little door in the back of each cage leading to "Ape Island" so an ape can escape to frolic in the sunshine among the trees with his ape family and friends. Subjecting apes to the same conditions we routinely design for people would be considered animal abuse. In most northern European countries, codes require that every employee desk be located within 7 meters (about 21 feet) of a window. In comparison, many US workers spend all day without glimpsing the world outside. People need Ape Islands too. Isn't that why we plan vacations to beaches, lakes, mountains and national parks?

> *Patients recovering from abdominal surgery recovered faster, had better emotional well-being, and required fewer strong pain medications if they had bedside windows with a nature view (looking out onto trees) than if their windows looked out onto a brick wall.*
>   *(Ulrich 1984)*

> *Cimprich (1992) reported greater gains in recovering cancer patients who carried out nature activities (three times a week for about half an hour at a time) than in members of a comparison group.*
>   Rachel Kaplan, Stephen Kaplan, and Robert L. Ryan, <u>With People in Mind</u>

> *Hungering, hungering, hungering for primal energies and Nature's dauntlessness.*
>   Walt Whitman, 1865

The Hidden Messages in earlier chapters describe floor patterns and relationships based upon human instinct and what we see in nature. This chapter moves into the world we can touch; natural materials (and their look-and-feel-a-likes).

II. FLOORING MATERIALS AND PATTERNS THAT TAKE INSPIRATION FROM NURTURING ELEMENTS IN NATURE CREATE POSITIVE HEALTH OUTCOMES

> *#247   Paving with Cracks between the Stones*
> *Asphalt and concrete surfaces outdoors are easy to wash (and walk on), but they do nothing for us, nothing for the paths, and nothing for the rainwater and plants... (when) you walk from stone to stone, you feel the earth directly under your feet...*
>   Christopher Alexander, <u>A Pattern Language</u>

> *Natural materials bring us back into alignment with our own inner nature. This sense of groundedness is fundamental in reducing stress, elevating melatonin, and promoting strong immune systems to support health and well-being. Most of us are aware of the therapeutic benefit of walking barefoot on a beach: natural flooring materials have a similar effect on our psyche as well as our bodies.*
>   Alex Stark, Feng Shui Consultant

Organic Flooring Materials and Patterns

Natural materials and patterns like wood, bamboo, brick and stone are greatly appreciated - even by city dwellers more familiar with concrete, carpet and ceramic tile (and to people who live in extreme icy or arid climates and never walk on paths strewn with autumn leaves). Studies show that the materials we select for buildings can change the behavior and expectations of occupants as well as people just viewing a building.

> *Building materials influence judgments about the occupants, too. In one study, observers were shown houses made of brick, concrete block, weathered wood, stucco, flagstone and wooden shingles.*
> *Residents of concrete block houses were seen as cold and non-artistic and residents of wooden shingle houses were seen as warm and creative.*
> Robert Gifford, <u>Environmental Psychology Principles and Practice</u>

If you want to appeal to the largest number of people, then ask yourself these questions before selecting final floor materials, colors and textures,

"What does this pattern or material remind me of? Someplace I want to be?"
- *Like a forest in the spring? (a hardwood-patterned floor)*
- *Or a sandy beach? (smooth rounded pebbles on the shower floor)*

"Or someplace I don't really want to be?"
- *Like a factory? (cracked, stained concrete flooring in condominiums)*

Make sure that your design decisions follow your intentions. Remember to avoid "design-speak" since your end-users (unlike you) will react instinctively based upon how the space feels to them - its "spirit".

> *The latest science leads us to a worldview not unlike that held by the earliest civilizations, in which every material object in nature was thought to possess a spirit. Aboriginal cultures do not make the usual distinctions among rocks, air and humans; all are imbued with spirit, the invisible energy. Doesn't that sound familiar? This is the world of <u>quantum physics</u>, in which matter and energy are entirely entangled.*
> Bruce H. Lipton, Ph.D. <u>The Biology of Belief</u>

Natural Materials vs. Imitations

Surprisingly, research studies show that images and materials don't need to be real in order to help reduce stress. Our ancestors (the ones whose instincts we inherited along with their DNA) knew nothing about photographs or paintings. In their world, if it looked like a plant then it <u>was</u>

a plant. Today, whether we look at a natural or artificial Christmas tree, the same feelings are triggered. That's good news since it means that we can specify natural materials and hi-quality imitators to give people a psychological and physical boost in urban and extreme environments.

> ...*strong evidence that even fairly brief encounters with real **or simulated** nature settings can elicit significant recovery from stress within three minutes to five minutes at most.*
> *(Parsons and Hartig, 2000; Ulrich, 1999)*

Today the flooring industry is pushing this concept in new directions with a variety of hard and soft surface materials that look (and feel) like wood, stone and other natural elements. This trend is healthy. Because our preference for natural colors and materials is based upon human instinct and does positive things for us physically and psychologically, it will likely continue to be much more than just a trend.

> *Go to the woods and fields for color schemes.*
> Frank Lloyd Wright

Nature-Inspired Flooring for my own Clients

As an Architect and Interior Designer working with corporations and professional firms in the San Francisco Bay Area, I consistently recommend flooring that brings the colors and patterns of nature inside buildings. I feel strongly that the best flooring choice is most often the one that reminds us of the ground outside.

The following examples are part of larger stories about how I try to balance the energies in building design from site planning through furniture specification using instinct and nature-based research to recommend building shapes, massing, materials, colors, wall, floor and ceiling finishes, furniture and artwork.

■   **The San Francisco Office of the New York Times**
My client leased a floor in a high-rise building high above adjacent buildings. The staff was surrounded by perimeter walls of glass and by blue sky. No trees or plants were visible unless someone walked to the window and looked directly down. In order to "ground" the space and staff I could have recommended earth colors (like terracotta, gold or taupe). But as you've read in studies earlier in this book, green is the color that is most associated with creativity by current scientific research as well as ancient cultures. The staff members are predominantly writers, photographers and graphic designers so the Bureau Chief agreed that a green creativity-enhancing carpet would be the best choice.

What carpet did he select? An organic pattern appropriately named Prairie Grass in the color Meadow. (See Figure 9.1)

■   **The Rubin Family Vineyards and Winery**
My client and his wife purchased a winery in Sonoma County, California to develop their own wines, and decided to rebuild the Hospitality Rooms and Offices adjacent to the Cellar that housed hundreds of barrels of wine. This is a working winery surrounded by lush green vineyards and rolling hills – more than enough green for any creative spirit.

The earth that the vineyard workers, winemakers and visitors would unintentionally bring into the building every time they stepped inside is a light gold color (aptly named Goldridge soil). So we selected stone-patterned 12 x 24 porcelain tiles in the corridors and Break Room to match this earth color. The carpet in the offices areas needed to include the same light gold to hide footprints, but too much of this color would be a carpet-cleaning nightmare. We needed contrast, so my clients approved an elegant black and gold carpet in an organic woven raffia pattern. Ron and Pam agreed that both the flooring (black and pale gold) and the furniture (ebony and ash) could contribute to a balanced dark/light, Yin/Yang energy that would provide the most auspicious and healthy beginning to their wine country adventure. (See Figure 9.2)

■ American Institute of Architects San Francisco Office

A few years ago when I was asked to help design the interiors of the new AIA chapter office, I realized this would be a challenge. After all, architects love the combination of white, grey, charcoal and black – with a touch of red. I would need to pull the chapter's board of directors kicking and screaming into nature-based colors and patterns (regardless of the importance of sustainability, LEED and everything 'green').

So I decided to push them very slightly – I know my people. The carpet tile selected and installed is a very dark textured grey-green on grey-green in a large stone pattern (almost charcoal if you squint your eyes). Some of the "whites" in the space became "linens", and the "red" accents became "deep orange" accents – little victories.
(See Figure 9.3)

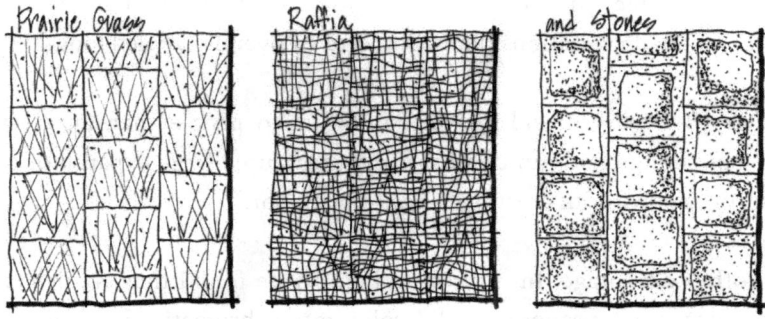

Figure 9.1   **Figure 9.2**   **Figure 9.3**
A few of the patterns and colors from nature that can ground interior spaces

The three carpets I just described all include organic patterns (meadow grass, woven raffia, and large stones). I wasn't trying to lead people anywhere so energy outcomes became my primary goal in carpet selection. The following are other natural patterns I've recommended as a consultant when I work with architectural and interior design firms after building owners decide they want a nature and research-based approach.

Dappled-Light Floor Patterns

> We enjoy being in dappled light (Wise and Hubbard 2000)... probably because during our ancient past when we were experiencing it, we were relaxed because the weather was good and because we had a quick means of escape (up the tree casting those irregular shadows) if we saw danger approaching.
> Sally Augustin PhD,
> <u>Place Advantage: Applied Psychology for Interior Architecture</u>

Floor patterns created in both hard and soft surfaces can imitate the pleasurable experience of walking in dappled light in three ways:

- As part of an overall pattern when you purposely specify a blend of differently colored tiles in the same pattern or style.
- When you choose tiles or materials with a wide variation of color, shading and pattern within one style/color specification.
- When you select flooring material large enough to include shade variations that will create an overall dappled look.

A dappled pattern will feel more natural to people than an arbitrary graphic design and can often visually break up a large expanse of corridor or area without creating "lines on the floor."

Another advantage: In my consulting, I have found that architects and designers who propose a solid-color monochromatic floor as part of their minimalist Schematic Design are more open to the "dappled light" concept than to breaking up a large corridor or space (for the reasons already described in this book) with a bolder more identifiable and literally interpreted pattern from nature.

> Recent research indicates that paths that travel through garden areas or even along corridors with shadowing and mottling... seem to have a calming effect on dementia sufferers.
> (Zeisel, J. 2005)

Wood Patterned Flooring

People like the color, grain, texture and feeling of hardwood flooring because it unconsciously reminds us of walking on forest paths. Wood flooring has been the most common residential flooring material in cultures throughout the world since our ancestors decided that dirt floors made their homes – well, too "dirty."

Home improvement programs confirm our instinctive preference for wood flooring when:
- "Sell This House" designers are thrilled when they rip up old 1970's shag carpet to find hardwood flooring in <u>any</u> condition.
- "Househunters" homebuyers accept plastic laminate wood-patterned flooring and wood engineered flooring, but are happiest with hardwood (even when they can't tell the difference).

FLOOR FOCUS Magazine noted in 2014 that as much as 30% of the ceramic and porcelain tile market is "wood look." Vinyl and plastic laminate wood patterns are also increasingly popular. These materials recreate hardwoods as well as distressed and exotic wood patterns and colors. Additionally, at least 60% of tile sizes (in all materials) now have a rectangular or plank shape. People <u>like</u> wood!

> *Wood provides stress-reducing effects similar to the well-studied effect of exposure to nature in the field of environmental psychology... Wood may be able to be applied indoors to provide stress reduction as a part of the evidence-based and biophilic design of hospitals, offices, schools, and other built environments.*
>   *(David Fell, 2010)*

> *This information is particularly important because wood can be used in any sort of space—for example ones without views of nature or ones that cannot support plants. The wood included in the test environment was birch veneer office furniture with a clear finish.*
>   *Research Design Connections, 2013, Issue 1*

Stone, Bamboo and Cork Materials and Patterns

Real Estate Agents (and everyone who has watched an HGTV program in the last five years) know how <u>absolutely necessary</u> stone (granite, quartzite, etc.) countertops are to the happiness of potential buyers. *(That's one reason why I don't design houses – I don't have the strength to deal with people who say they NEED something that 99.9% of humanity doesn't have, and that they actually just WANT).* Plastic laminate counters with granite or marble patterns are the second choice. But back to flooring...

Bamboo, cork, marble, granite and slate are other natural materials that are popularly used as flooring. The same patterns in other materials like LVT, plastic laminate and porcelain are increasingly popular since new technology allows those materials to capture the look, variation, texture and feel of the natural materials they imitate. This preference for using natural and natural-looking materials is driven equally by end-users as by designers.

> *Some of our responses are inborn. Somehow certain sorts of experiences affect people in different parts of the world in the same way, and have for generations.*
>   *(Kellert, 2005)*

Anyone who has ever taken an Architectural History class knows that using industrial-looking flooring in all types of projects was triggered by Bauhaus designers and 20th-century modern manufacturing techniques.

Industrial flooring, including large expanses of solid-color flooring, is a design choice that has never been as popular among the general public as it is with design-professionals.

Question: Why don't end-users like "expanses of solid-colors?"

Answer: Because they don't include fractals....

What's a Fractal??????

When I started reading about fractals, I felt exactly the same way I did the night I went to the landscaping seminar and learned about cliffing.

> *"How can I have been an Architect and Interior Designer for decades and not have heard ANYTHING about fractals? Where have I been?"*

In case you've missed all the talk about fractals too, here's my simple explanation; when you look at a fence covered entirely by green vines, the overall image is green but the vines are made up of leaves with millions of slightly different shapes, sizes and colors (fractals). Every scene in nature contains this complexity and detail that changes as the sun's position changes in the sky - constant variation.

> *We find it soothing to look at certain patterns that are mathematically similar to ones that occur in nature. These patterns are called natural fractals, and they are present in a field of grass that is being gently rippled by the wind clouds moving across the sky, or a winding stream...fish tank ripples, dappled light...The calm mental state induced by these sorts of patterns has been found to spur creative, high energy mental activity.*
>   Sally Augustin PhD,
>   <u>Place Advantage: Applied Psychology for Interior Architecture</u>

My Living Room has a wood-plank ceiling (as do many vacation homes, log cabins and A-Frames around the country). Wood ceilings subconsciously remind us of forest canopies: freedom, fresh air and tree houses! But painting a standard ceiling the same color brown would feel oppressive and drab. (How many brown-painted ceilings have <u>you</u> seen?)

> *In our evolutionary past, the forest was a timepiece with colors changing hour by hour as the sun arched across the sky. Since then, designers have pledged allegiance to unchanging dye lots, and the sameness of our interiors no longer makes sense to the deepest part of us.*
>   Janine Benyus in <u>Biophilic Design</u>

Solid-colored surfaces in flooring and painted walls don't have fractals. Most of our building interiors have smooth surfaces and constant lighting because those are the least expensive to construct. Painting an accent wall apple green doesn't give us the same health benefit as looking at a fence with vines (although including a green accent wall is still psychologically better for people far from windows than all beige, grey or white walls). Anyway, only modern machines can make totally uniform flooring. It couldn't happen before the Industrial Revolution so it doesn't do anything for us instinctively and psychologically.

This gets back to the Monochromatic Bubble chapter where I wrote that only the <u>dangerous</u> natural environments were one color (like sandstorms and snowstorms). At least sand and snow are made up of fractals! According to current research they would feel more normal to us than standing in a large room with perfectly painted one-color walls and a one-color vinyl floor. (More "life in outer space" than "life on Earth"?)

People are instinctively more comfortable in an environment with fractals. That's one reason why we love Tuscan hill-towns and old world wood, brick and stone cities built with uneven and imperfect finishes and surfaces. We take hundreds of photographs and then come home to specify perfectly consistent finishes on our own projects.

> *Another study identified more cooperative behaviors among children in day-care centers where rooms had varied wall color as opposed to uniformity.*
> *Pelligrini, A.D. Journal of Applied Developmental Psychology 1985*

> *Scientific research has shown that when people see or hear fractal patterns like those found in nature, they are more relaxed and devote less mental energy to monitoring their environment; fractals are variations on a theme... and produce the sorts of backgrounds against which primitive humans could have easily spotted approaching danger, such as lions or tigers or bears.*
> *(Wise and Hazzard, 2002)*

Green Grass Fractals

As a Consultant on a variety of project types, I always recommend one fractal solution for boring grey flat roofs that are seen by people looking down from the upper floors of a building complex. My recommendation? Artificial grass.

Generally the architects respond that they had already proposed a Green Roof for that area but that it had been value-engineered-out due to the higher structural, irrigation, and landscape maintenance costs. Designers seem troubled by my (then repeated multiple times) recommendation to skip the higher cost "Green Roof System" and just install less expensive artificial turf. It's not real. But it's green. And it has "Fractals".

> ...Only in very recent times have we begun to fill our landscapes with other colors, ...reflective glass and gunmetal steel, red bricks and gray concrete... (Green) was the background we were weaned on in primordial times, the background that told us we were safe...lulled us to sleep against a darkening sky.
> Dr. Esther M. Sternberg, <u>Healing Spaces</u>

We see fields of artificial green grass on high school football, baseball and soccer fields around the country so people are used to the look. Why not use artificial grass on highly visible roof decks? With stone-shaped light-colored pavers to increase the park look and add a lighter color for less solar absorption? Then building occupants would get a similar psychological lift to what they would experience looking down at a park (according to research proving that simulating nature also produces positive health outcomes). It is becoming more common to install artificial rivers and riverbanks using small colored stones on roof decks visible from patient rooms in some new healthcare complexes in milder climates like California.

I haven't ever proposed just painting a roof grass-green (although that would still be better than adding another grey roof to a city landscape unless solar reflectance is a concern). But painting a roof green would really cause architectural eyeballs to roll, and a painted roof would still be missing one very important feature of artificial grass (those fractals).

> People experiencing natural fractals thus have more mental processing power available for valued activities such as being creative, monitoring details, and interacting with others. The experience of natural fractals has been shown to speed recovery from surgery and to increase office worker productivity.
>
> Research on knowledge-worker offices has shown that the use of natural fractals in an environment can improve memory while reducing stress and keeping cognitive performance from deteriorating over time.
> Research Design Connections, 2013, issue 1

Residential Fractals

Residential Kitchens and Bathrooms are increasingly full of fractals since they are designed with many more tiles than they were in the past. The more expensive the house, the more natural materials in fractal patterns and pieces everywhere:

- DIY's can buy hundreds of glittering glass ½" tiles on backing strips at Home Depot for easy backsplash installation.
- Subway Tile wainscot seems to have replaced painted dry wall with high wood base as the standard in Bathroom Designs.
- Showrooms display hundreds of floor accent tiles in intricate patterns and color combinations that add detail to field tile.
- Porcelain tiles (which in the past were used primarily in monochromatic hi-tech designs) include stone, slate and wood patterns in multiple sizes, textures and colors that are installed on counters and floors.
- Smooth rounded stones in a variety of colors and sizes are used on shower walls and floors.
- Wood planks (in every material) vary from plank to plank to purposely recreate the fractal inconsistencies in hardwood.

> *Branching, self-similar patterns that occur repeatedly at increasingly smaller scales are found throughout nature, not only in trees but also in waves, snowflakes, seashells, and flowers...We don't know why repeating patterns are pleasing to the eye, but perhaps their existence in the natural world accounts, in part, for the calming influence of nature views.*
> Dr. Esther M. Sternberg, <u>Healing Spaces</u>

III.   FLOORING MATERIALS AND PATTERNS THAT TAKE INSPIRATION FROM <u>NON-NURTURING</u> ELEMENTS IN NATURE

When you design and specify flooring, remember that - regardless of my never-ending "back to nature" mantra - people aren't comfortable <u>everywhere</u> in nature. The natural world can be dangerous and depressing!

I was surprised a few years ago to see that a carpet tile patterned and colored to look like stained and moldy concrete had won a healthcare design award at Neocon! That was another case where my design-mind said, *"Very cool urban-grunge-looking pattern. How did they do that?"* while my Ethel-from-Modesto avatar said, *"Why does that carpet look so <u>dirty</u>?")*

The Matte vs. Glossy Debate in Healthcare Facilities and other examples of literal thinking becoming literal feelings

I saw the award-winning grunge pattern at the same time that my own healthcare clients were telling me that many hospital staff members still believed that a floor needs to have a high-gloss finish to look clean. The following questions relate to literal thinking and pre-conceptions that influence flooring material selection:

Does the color-shading in that tile purposely make the floor look dirty?
Does that pattern purposely make the floor look like it's cracking?

Does that finish purposely make the floor look slippery?
How would that floor look to Conan or Ayla who knew nothing about "floors"?

Many of my corporate clients initially love the idea of exposed concrete floors in their Lobby and Reception Areas. It can be a great look for a lower cost. But what appears compelling in design magazines doesn't look quite the same to them when they step off the elevator and say,

"But this floor has a lot of cracks – is it safe?
We're in California. What will happen in an earthquake?"

It doesn't seem to help when I say that concrete floors are safe and always have cracks. Then I tell them that if their First Impression leaving the elevator every morning makes them feel insecure and worry about earthquakes, then it's not setting them up for a great day! So we're back to tile, wood or carpet.

Shiny floors can be just as unsettling as cracking floors (except to hospital staff – it gets back to education and experience). People understand that a shiny glaring surface in nature is either icy or wet (and slippery). We subconsciously connect glossy floors with slipping and falling. Approaching a shiny floor is just one more thing to worry about to someone afraid of slipping and falling for any reason, like the sick or elderly, a skier with a bum knee or a gorgeous 20-something on 4" stiletto heels.

> ...the glossier the surface the greater the glare, which can cause temporary blindness and pain and may create a false perception of elevation change or of a solid obstacle.
> Dak Kopec, *Environmental Psychology for Design*

A matte finish is a less stressful choice than a glossy finish psychologically. If it looks like a safe ground surface in nature (like a path with a pebbly texture), then people instinctively feel more comfortable and are less likely to tense their bodies which could trigger a fall. For that and other reasons, carpet is increasingly being used in healthcare facilities. The following studies give some pros and cons of both types of flooring:

> ...carpeting, compared to hard floorings, offers important advantages unrelated to infection control, including noise reduction (Philbin and Gray, 2002)
>
> ...greater ease of walking and perceived safety for the elderly (Wilmott, 1986)
>
> ...a possible reduction in falls (Counsell et al., 2000)
>
> ...longer family visits in patient rooms and more positive evaluations and emotional responses from patients and families (Harris, 2000)
>
> ...however, carpeting should be avoided in areas where spills are likely to occur or where patients are at greater risk of airborne infections (Sehulster et al., 2004)

> "A Review of the Research Literature on Evidence-Based Healthcare Design"
> HERD, Vol.1, No.3

IN THIS CHAPTER YOU LEARNED THAT UNLESS YOUR CLIENT'S GOALS WILL REQUIRE A DIFFERENT STRATEGY, YOU WILL HELP THEM MOST BY SPECIFYING NATURAL (OR NATURAL-<u>LOOKING</u>) FLOORING MATERIALS.

> *Treat nature as a model and mentor, not an inconvenience to be evaded or controlled.*
> William McDonough

> *The floors we walk on are embodiments of our deepest connection to the earth, nature and its landscapes. The more natural the material, the closer we will feel connected to the nourishing qualities of familiar landscapes. This connection is not only visual, it also depends on the tactile, olfactory, and sound qualities of these materials.*
> Alex Stark, Feng Shui Consultant

The old Lakota was wise. He knew that man's heart away from nature becomes hard.
    Luther Standing Bear, Oglala Sioux

I believe in God, only I spell it Nature.
    Frank Lloyd Wright

SUMMARY

You don't need to follow these Hidden Message concepts blindly... but it would be good to consider them your default position.

If you have a good reason to design differently, then do! But question your reasons for not complying with human instinct and the patterns in nature that humans have preferred for thousands of years.

It's too easy for architects to fall under the starchitect spell and follow the "Architecture as Art and Sculpture" approach to design. It goes against our training to think that new and different isn't always better; but that seems to be the case when it comes to human comfort.

> *Architects pretend to have surpassed human nature. Instead, certain formal and abstract notions about space, materials, and form are of primary concern. Those do not arise, however, from a full understanding of the processes at work that give human beings their existential foothold on earth.*
> *Nikos Salingaros and Kenneth Masden II in* Biophilic Design

If you are the lead designer on a project – Congratulations!

You can apply your own design style, using the Hidden Message concepts during Design Development when you select materials and develop patterns. In most cases, following the recommendations in this book will simplify patterns since new seaming technology for both hard and soft surfacing has resulted in some inexplicably complex floor designs.

Reducing complexity will also save your client money. Be sure to point THAT out while explaining how your design will promote their goals. *(One of my floor pattern recommendations saved my healthcare client more than $40,000 by reducing seaming costs over seven floors of patient rooms.)*

And if you are not (yet) the Lead Designer on a project?

If you have a client (or are working with a more senior designer) whose own ideas are headed in the Creative-Innovation Based direction instead of the end-users' Instinctive–Experiential Based direction, then this is the strategy I've found to be most effective with my own clients and their project design teams:

1. When it's time to develop flooring ideas for your project, determine your phase in the design process. There is nothing that will kill your credibility faster than making a recommendation after "that ship has sailed" and implementing a specific research-based concept that would increase the project budget or schedule. Accept past design decisions, and take it forward.

2. Say, *"Studies show xxxxxxx"* (describing a benefit to the end-user or client) and then make your specific design recommendation. The studies noted in this book are the ones I reference most frequently during the design process, creatively extrapolating the information depending upon the project phase and the specific design options.

3. Then step back. If a more senior designer or the client disagrees with your research-based design recommendation, then that is their choice. You'll feel confident and happier just knowing that your recommendation came from a place of Service.

Generally, my clients agree with me because they like having a stated purpose behind design proposals. Architects and Interior Designers may or may not be interested in this approach, depending upon their mindset. You may be "designing with a purpose" but that doesn't mean your ideas will prevail. There are many times when I feel like a tugboat trying to turn the Queen Mary. But I consider any movement in the nature and instinct direction a success because it will impact end-users positively.

One major benefit of incorporating nature and instinct-based research: You can avoid design-ego battles!

IT FEELS FABULOUS avoiding the tricky "my design idea is better than your design idea" discussions that sometimes happen when designers on the same project team try to convince each other which direction to take. When a client asks me to work with their designers, my role is to propose a design approach for every major design decision based upon research. I must leave the specific design interpretation and details to the project designers and their creative vision. That is their job.

As you've learned in previous chapters, the Hidden Messages don't dictate design style. Designers can take these flooring ideas and move in a variety of directions within their overall project design concept. But the end design result will not be based solely upon a passing trend or ego.

> *Until you transcend the ego, you can do nothing but add to the insanity of the world. That statement should delight you rather than create despair, for it removes the burden from your shoulders.*
>
> John Randolph Price, A Spiritual Philosophy for the New World

My Final (not just about flooring) Thoughts

Most of us (honestly) do not have clients who want cutting-edge award-winning design. Most of us have clients who want to spend happier and healthier lives in comfortable and aesthetically pleasing buildings that will promote their goals and that they will be proud to call theirs.

And clients with every project type increasingly want to help people while helping our planet.

Our goal should not be creating "good design" (an ever-changing description that is always open to debate – especially with more than three designers in a room). We should be creating "places that are good for people." Those will be the places that people will want to occupy and maintain far into the future. That is the very definition of sustainability.

> *The most sustainable building is the one that's loved.*
> *Cameron Sinclair, CEO Architecture for Humanity*
> *AIA National Convention in Denver, 2013*

The main thing I've learned after years of applying psychology-related research to design is that we all instinctively understand more than we recognize about which places are best for us.

We just need to <u>feel</u> a little more – and <u>think</u> a little less.

> *My guess is that good places feel right and that spills over to the staff, the body language, the voices, the vase of flowers – magic happens at places like that.*
> *Derek Parker, FAIA, RIBA, FACHA*

BIBLIOGRAPHY

Author Notes:
1. The books, publications and websites noted below with the symbol ■ are great "next step" resources for readers interested in pursuing practical "read something today that you can use tomorrow" research.

2. Research studies quoted throughout the text and noted like this: *(researcher's name, date)* are not attributed to one book because the same studies are mentioned in many of the resources noted below.

3. The resources below informed my 3-Part 18-Principle Architectural Design Psychology System that relates to <u>all</u> phases of design from Site Planning and Building Design through Art Selection, not exclusively to Flooring.

Television Programs and Websites

HGTV Programs:	Designed to Sell + Get It Sold + Househunters
A&E Programs:	Sell This House + Flip This House
TLC Programs:	Property Ladder

■ https://www.ArchitecturalDesignPsychology.com/
The author's website includes additional information and resources.

■ https://www.InformeDesign.org/
On this free website, more than 2,400 research summaries from peer-reviewed journals link design and human behavior in a variety of project type settings.

- https://www.healthdesign.org/
The Center for Health Design website provides tools and resources for healthcare professionals and organizations including the Knowledge Repository, a centerpiece for all healthcare design research, papers, articles and references, along with evidence-based design accreditation and certification, (EDAC), information and educational offerings.

- https://www. ResearchDesignConnections.com/
This site combines an extensive collection of practical articles and blog-posts where you can search for specific design-related keywords for all project types.

- http://www.healthdesign.org/chd/research/role-physical-environment-hospital-21st-century
The Role of the Physical Environment in the Hospital of the 21st Century: A Once-in-a-Lifetime Opportunity
This is a great free report to download, packed with evidence-based design studies by Roger Ulrich, Xiaobo Quan, Craig Zimring, Anjali Joseph, Ruchi Choudhary, and funded by the Robert Wood Johnson Foundation in 2004.

Flooring Information Sources

Floor FOCUS	https://www. floordaily.net
Floor Covering Weekly	https://www. floorcoveringweekly.com

Books and Publications

Alexander, Christopher. *A Pattern Language.* New York: Oxford University Press, 1977.

Alexander, Christopher. *The Timeless Way of Building.* New York: Oxford University Press, 1979.

Anderson, Richard Feather. "The Mastery Spiral: A Celtic Geomancy Wheel." 2006

- Augustin, Sally, PhD. *Place Advantage: Applied Psychology for Interior Architecture.* Hoboken, New Jersey: John Wiley & Sons, Inc., 2009.

Barker, Roger. *Ecological Psychology: Concepts and Methods for Studying the Environment of Human Behavior.* Stanford: Stanford University Press, 1968.

Baum, Andrew, and Jerome E. Singer. *Advances in Environmental Psychology: Volume 4 Environment and Health.* New Jersey: Lawrence Erlbaum Associates, Publishers, 1982.

Bell, Paul, Thomas Greene, Jeffrey Fisher and Andrew Baum. *Environmental Psychology*, 5th ed. Belmont, CA: Wadsworth Group/Thomson Learning, 2001.

Birren, Faber. *Color & Human Response.* New York: John Wiley & Sons, 1978.

Cama, Rosalyn. *Evidence-Based Healthcare Design.* Hoboken, New Jersey: John Wiley & Sons, Inc., 2009.

Carr-Gomm, Philip. *The Elements of The Druid Tradition.* Great Britain: Element Books Limited, 1993.

The Center for Health Design. *An Introduction to Evidence Based Design.* Concord, CA: CHD, 2008.

Cowan, James G. *The Elements of The Aborigine Tradition.* Great Britain: Element Books Limited, 1992.

Cox, Kathleen. *The Power of Vastu Living.* New York, NY: Fireside, 2002.

Cox, Kathleen. *Vastu Living.* New York: Marlowe and Company, 2000.

Day, Christopher. *Places of the Soul.* London: Thorsons, 1993.

Dwivedi, Dr. Manjul Kant. *Remedial Vastu: Harmony with Nature for Peace, Health & Prosperity.* Lucknow, India: International Society, 2008.

Evans, Dylan and Oscar Zarate. *Introducing Evolutionary Psychology.* Lanham, MD: Totem Books, 2000.

Gallagher, Winifred. *House Thinking: A Room-by-Room Look at How We Live.* New York: Harper-Collins, 2006.

Gallagher, Winifred, *The Power of Place: How Our Surroundings Shape Our Thoughts, Emotions and Actions.* New York: Harper Perennial, 2007.

Gifford, Robert. *Environmental Psychology Principles and Practice.* Needham Heights, MA: Allyn and Bacon, 1997.

Goodman, Ted (edited by). *The Forbes Book of Business Quotations.* New York: Black Dog and Leventhal, 1997.

Herman Miller. *See: The Potential of Place.* Issue 4, Spring 2006.

Hobday, Richard. *The Healing Sun, Sunlight and Health in the 21st Century.* Finland: Findhorn Press, 1999.

Holmes, Ann Marie. *Earth Spirit Living.* Hillsboro, OR: Atria Books/Beyond Words Publishing, 2006.

Hyder, Carol J. *Wind and Water: Your Personal Feng Shui Journey.* Freedom, CA: Crossing Press, 1998.

Ittelson, William., Harold Proshansky, Leanne Rivlin, and Gary Winkel. *An Introduction to Environmental Psychology.* New York: Holt, Rinehart and Winston, Inc., 1974.

Kaplan, Rachel, Stephen Kaplan, and Robert L. Ryan. *With People in Mind: Design and Management of Everyday Nature.* Washington D.C.: Island Press, 1998.

■ Kellert, Stephen, Judith Heerwagen, and Martin Mador. *Biophilic Design.* Hoboken, NJ: John Wiley & Sons, 2008.

■ Kopec, Dak. *Environmental Psychology for Design.* New York: Fairchild Publications, Inc. 2006.

Krishna, Talavane, M.D. *The Vaastu Workbook.* Vermont: Destiny Books, 2001.

Lawlor, Anthony. *The Temple in the House: Finding the Sacred in Everyday Architecture.* New York: G.P. Putnam's Son's, 1994.

■ Leibrock, Cynthia, and Debra Harris. *Design Details for Health.* 2nd ed. Hoboken, NJ: John Wiley & Sons, 2011.

Liberman, Jacob, O.D, Ph.D. *Light, Medicine of the Future.* Santa Fe, NM: Bear & Company, 1991.

Lipton, Bruce H., PhD., *The Biology of Belief.* Carlsbad, CA: Hay House, Inc., 2013.

Magee, Vishu. *Archetype Design: House as a Vehicle for Spirit.* Taos, NM: Archetype Design Publications, 1999.

Marcus, Clare Cooper. *House as a Mirror of Self.* Berkeley, CA: Conari Press, 1997.

Matthews, Caitlin. *The Elements of The Celtic Tradition.* Great Britain: Element Books Limited, 1998.

Michell, John. *The New View Over Atlantis.* London: Thames and Hudson Ltd, 1983.

Nabokov, Peter and Robert Easton. *Native American Architecture.* New York: Oxford University Press, 1989.

Nanda, U., Chanaud, C., Nelson, M., Zhu, X., Bajema, R., Jansen, B.H. (2012) "Impact of Visual Art on Patient Behavior in the Emergency Department Waiting Room," The Journal of Emergency Medicine Vol.43

Nanda, U., Malone, E., and Joseph, A. (2012) "Achieving Evidence Based Design Goals through Flooring Selection and Design", Concord, CA: The Center for Health Design.

Ott, John N. *Health and Light.* Columbus, OH: Ariel Press, 1976.

Ozaniec, Naomi. *The Elements of Egyptian Wisdom.* Great Britain: Element Books Limited, 1998.

Pennick, Nigel. *Earth Harmony: Places of Power, Holiness and Healing.* Berks, England: Capall Bann Publishing, 1997.

Pollio, Marcus Vitruvius translated by Morris Hicky Morgan. *The Ten Books on Architecture.* New York: Dover Publications, 1960.
Post, Steven. *The Modern Book of Feng Shui.* New York: Byron Press, 1998.

Rossbach, Sarah. *Feng Shui: The Chinese Art of Placement.* New York: Penguin Compass, 2000.

Rossbach, Sarah. *Interior Design with Feng Shui.* New York: Penguin Compass, 2000.

Sahasrabudhe, N.H. and R.D.Mahatme, *Secrets of Vastushastra.* New Delhi, India: Sterling Publishers Ltd., 1999.

Salingaros, Nikos A. *Unified Architectural Theory: Form, Language, Complexity – A Companion to Christopher Alexander's The Phenomenon of Life, The Nature of Order; Book 1.* Vagira Books, 2013.

SantoPietro, Nancy. *Feng Shui and Health.* New York: Three Rivers Press, 2002.

Sommer, Robert. *Personal Space.* Englewood Cliffs, N.J.: Prentice-Hall, Inc., 1969.

Spear, William. *Feng Shui Made Easy.* New York: Harper Collins, 1995.

Smith, Vincent and Barbara Lyons Stewart. *Feng Shui: A Practical Guide for Architects and Designers.* Chicago, IL: Kaplan, 2006.

Steiner, Frederick. *Human Ecology: Following Nature's Lead.* Washington, D.C., Island Press, 2002.

Sternberg, Esther M., M.D. *Healing Spaces: The Science of Place and Well-Being.* Cambridge, MA: The Belknap Press of Harvard University, 2009.

Suzuki, David. *The Sacred Balance: Rediscovering Our Place in Nature.* Vancouver, BC: Greystone Books, 2002.

Swann, James A. *The Power of Place: Sacred Ground in Natural & Human Environments.* Wheaton, IL: Quest Books, 1991.

Thompson, Angel. *Feng Shui: How to Achieve the Most Harmonious Arrangement of your Home or Office.* New York: St. Marin's Press, 1996.

Underhill, Paco. *Call of the Mall: The Geography of Shopping.* New York: Simon & Schuster, 2004.

Underhill, Paco. *Why We Buy: The Science of Shopping.* New York: Simon & Schuster, 1999.

Vendome Group and The Center for Health Design, *HERD Health Environments Research & Design Journal,* Spring 2008 Vol.1, No.3. LLC Publication.

Versluis, Arthur. *Native American Traditions.* Great Britain: Element Books Limited, 1994.

Whelan, Bilkis. *Vastu in 10 Simple Lessons.* New York: Watson-Guptill Publications, 2002.

Winston, Robert. *Human Instinct.* London: Bantam Books, 2002.

Winter, Deborah DuNann. *Ecological Psychology: Healing the Split between Planet and Self.* Psychology Press, 2002.

Wong, Eva. *A Master Course in Feng-Shui.* Boston: Shambhala Publications 2001.

Zeisel, John. *Inquiry by Design: Environmental/Behavior/Neuroscience in Architecture, Interiors, Landscape, and Planning.* New York: W. W. Norton & Company, 2006.

INDEX

18 Instinct-Based Design Principles

3-Part System, 21, 191

A

Aboriginal, 90, 170

Abstract art, 137-38, 159, 162

Abstract patterns, 158

Adrenaline, 8

Aesthetics, 11-12, 41

Africa, 16-18, 21, 153

Age, 16-17, 38, 54-55, 68, 74, 154

Airport, 112

Aisle, 75-76, *See also Corridor*

Alzheimer's, 25, 67, 154

Angled, Angular, *See also Diagonal* 79, 116, 136, 137

Animals, 16, 46, 90, 105, 120, 155-56, 160, 167

Anxiety, 8, 37, 45, 101, 147, 157

Apartment complex, 117

Appetite, 154

Applied Psychology, 3, 15, 127

Architects, 7, 11-13, 22, 53, 127, 173-174, 179, 185, 187

Architectural Design Psychology, 5, 12- 13, 14, 23, 42

Architectural determinism, 137

Architecture as art, 185

Area rug, 36-37, 59, 65-66, 163

Art, Artwork, 57, 59, 87, 101-102, 126, 137-38, 146, 162-63

Asian Compass School Feng Shui, 163

Asymmetrical, 81-85, 136-37, 160

Australia, 90

Avatar, 24, 64, 66, 71, 123, 125, 132, 139, 181

B

Balance, Balanced Energy, 48, 115, 140-46, 161-62

Bamboo, 111, 122, 123, 176

Bathroom, 64-65, 180

Bauhaus, 176

Bed, Bedroom, 36, 64, 65, 100, 163

Behavior, 15-17, 27, 29, 61, 80, 120-21

Benches, 109, 117

Biology, 19, 38, 40, 61, 155

Biophilia, Biophilic, 13, 15, 175-77

Borders, 80-86, 89, 94, 128

Brand, 55

Brick, 79, 168-69, 170, 178-79

Broadloom carpet, 31, 150, 161

Budget, 12-13, 57, 186

C

Cafeteria, 87, 121, 130

Calatrava, Santiago, 56

Carpet tile, 31, 114, 141-44, 173, 181

Casino designers, 132, 152

Caveman, 25, 71, 75

Center for Health Design (CHD), 9-10, 13-14

Centering, 75-87

Ceramic tile, 160

Checkerboard, 159

Chi, 89-90, 92, 93

China, 18-19, 35, 37, 90, 106, 135

Chronic stress, 8

Churches, 29

Circle of Life, 20, 167

Circles, Circular, 103, 107-108, 112, 117, 150-51

Classroom, 70, 81, 85, 121, 128

Client approval, satisfaction, 11, 42

Client goals, 42, 57-58, 114, 138

Cliffing, 73-87

CliffsNotes, 16

Clinic, 24, 70, 81, 121

Clutter, 149

Cognitive degeneration, 64

Colors and patterns, 61, 97, 127, 136-137, 139, 171

Colors, 45-61, 70, 95, 117, 125, 136-164, 171-3, 179

Commanding Position, 18

Conan the Barbarian, 25

Concentration, 11, 99, 135, 147

Concrete, 31, 74, 169, 170, 181-82

Conference table, 66-67

Contrast, 48-61, 70, 74, 79, 84, 95, 144, 156, 158-60

Cool colors, 136, 153-54

Cork, 176

Corporate, 11, 31, 39, 100, 139, 182

Corridor intersections, 111, 127-28, 132

Corridors (cliffing & centering) 73-87

Corridors (meandering) 110-113

Corridors (wayfinding) 125-133

Corridors (wind tunnel) 93-103

Creative Innovation-Based Perspective, 23

Creativity, 56, 141, 146, 148

Curves, Curvilinear, Curving, 106-113, 118, 136, 151

D

Dappled-light, 174

Depth Perception, 64

Design Approach and Process, 14, 143, 150, 152, 186

Design with a Purpose, 14, 40, 42, 57, 145, 187

Diagonal, 143-45, 151

Dining room table, 65-67

Djang, 90

Dog Park, 116-17

Doors, Doorways, 27, 67, 84, 108, 122, 124

Drop-off zone, 123-24

E

EBD, 9-11, 14-15, 33

EDAC, 10

Earth sciences, 19, 106

Eastern civilizations, 90

Ecology, 15, 38

Elevator bank, 58, 121, 131

Elevator cab, 31

End-users, 24, 57-59, 68, 70, 125, 138, 170

Energy, 35, 89-93, 136-164

Entrance, 28-31, 36-37, 109, 117, 121-24

Environmental Psychology, 15-16, 167

Evidence-Based Design, 9-10, 14-15

Evolutionary Biology, 15, 18

Evolutionary Psychologists, 15, 54

Eyes, Eyesight, 46, 48, 68, 74, 79, 80

F

Fabrics, 137, 151, 159, 162

Falling, 6, 7, 22, 63, 65, 182

Family, 163

Feng Shui, 18-19, 29, 36, 89, 92, 100, 115-16, 136, 163-64, 169, 183

Fight or Flight, 17

Finishes, 54, 57, 59, 143, 147, 159, 178

Fire, 47, 54-55

First Impression, 27-30, 34, 39-43

Flowers, 51, 79, 132, 181, 188

Floral, 61, 128

Forest, 46, 112, 120, 170, 175, 177

Form, 76, 112, 117, 124, 137, 185

Fractal, 177-180

Frog Story, 165

Function, 11, 66, 81, 125

Furniture, 18, 30, 35, 37, 57, 66, 79, 82, 102, 125, 137, 142, 147, 149, 159, 163

G

Gaia, 19, 106

Geomancy, 19, 106

Geometric pattern, 41

Glass, 100, 112, 115-16, 172, 180

Glossy, 181

Goals, 11-12, 14, 31, 37, 40-42, 58, 81, 114, 135, 138-39, 145-48, 151, 159, 161-62, 183, 188

Gothic Cathedrals, 56

Government, 29, 31

Grandmother Story, 63

Granites and marbles, 39, 176

Graphic design, 96, 122-24

Green, 13, 99, 117, 136, 146-48, 153-156, 177-180

Grounded, 45-48, 58-59

Grout, 95, 158

H

Habitat, 165

Hard and Soft flooring, 136

Hardwood, 47, 170, 175, 180

Healing gardens, 74, 79, 115

Healthcare Design, 10, 101, 181

Hearth, 25, 54-55

Hidden Messages, 22, 25, 41, 125, 187

Higher Energy Environment, 136, 141, 151

Horizontal & vertical, 78, 95, 137, 157

Hospital, 9, 64-67, 69, 84-85, 109, 119, 181-82

Hotel, 32, 75, 97, 147

House, 30, 47, 65, 92, 140, 147, 162-63, 175, 180

Human behavior, 16

Human instinct, 17, 19, 21, 46, 63, 120, 171, 185

I

ICU, 100

IIDA, 22

Illusion, 64, 68, 94, 159

Imbalanced, 102, 137, 146

Imitations, 170

Immune systems, 8, 169

India, 18-19, 35, 90

Industrial flooring, 176

Instinctive Experiential-Based, 20-21, 23, 62

Invisible energy, 90-91, 170

Iroquois, 90

J

Japan, 29, 38, 90

Johnson's Baby Center, 141-42

Joint, 62, 158

Judeo-Christian culture, 167

K

KTVU/FOX, 113-15

Ki, 90

L

Laboratory, 165

Landmark, 119, 126-33

Landscape Architect, 73, 79

Landscaping, 74, 116, 137, 148, 177

Law of Attraction, 35

Law Firm Story, 32, 161

Laws of Nature, 20

Lead Designer, 186

Light-is-Up, 46-47, 52-54, 58-59

Linear, 89, 94-95, 97-98, 101, 103

Line on the Ground, 61-63

Linoleum, 7, 31, 64, 158

Lobby, 31-32, 36-37, 39, 122, 182

LVT, 176

M

Manufacturers, v, 9, 68

Materials, 31, 39, 57, 67, 110, 116, 125, 136, 139, 169-71, 174-76, 183

Matte, 181

Meandering, 83, 105-118

Medical Laboratories, 147

Metal, 49, 115-16, 118, 147

Mexican restaurants, 152

Min Tang, "Bright Palace", 29

Minimalist Design, 137

Mirroring, 27, 35, 37

Monochromatic Bubbles, 49-59

Monolithic Tile Layout, 136

Multi-colored, 70, 136-37, 144

Multi-Purpose Room, 121, 130

Museums, 56

N

National Patient Safety Agency, 65, 71

Natural, Nature, 14, 17, 165-183

Neuroscience, 15, 53-55, 99

Nonslip flooring, 48, 65

North America, 90

Northern Europe, 90, 168

Novelty and originality, 53-54

Nurses Station, 86

O

Ond, 90

Open Houses, 30

Organic, 105, 117, 169

Orientation, 156-57, 162-63

P

Pain, 108, 182

Paris, 105-106

Park, 61, 117, 179

Parking, 109, 123, 126

Path, Pathways, 61, 75, 84, 93, 105-108, 110-12, 119-21, 123-24, 131

Patient, Patient Rooms, 9, 42, 64-65, 84-86, 97, 101, 159, 168, 179

Patterns, 5-6, 15, 21, 30, 61, 89, 105, 108, 119, 125, 136, 143, 155-56, 165, 169, 174, 181

Paving, 29, 31, 73-74, 79, 116-17, 122-123, 139, 169

Perspective, 16, 23, 25, 138

Photographs, 46, 49, 170

Plank shape, 175

Plants, 75-76, 90, 99, 105, 117, 155

Plastic laminate, 86, 175-76

Pneuma, 90

Prana, 90

Private offices, 31, 85, 161

Productivity, 11, 42, 135, 144

Programming, 32, 135, 138, 139, 161

Project type, 11, 31, 32, 67, 70, 85, 138, 188

Prospect and Refuge Theory, 17-18

Psychological Sustainability, 13

Public, 28-31, 84, 97

Q

Quantum physics, 35, 170

Quarter-Turn Tile Layout, 136

R

Real Estate Agents, 30, 47, 147

Reception Area, 31, 161

Rectangular, 112, 136-37

Rectilinear, 115

Rehabilitation, 49

Research-based design, 9, 11, 187

Residential, 67, 103, 175, 180

Rest Room, 31, 97

Retail, 55, 93, 108

Retention, 11

River Road Family Vineyards, 172

ROI (Return on Investment), 12

Rome, 47, 92, 105-106

Roof garden, 79

Roofs, 179

Rottet, Lauren, 57

Ruach, 90

Rubber, 80, 125, 129, 150

Runner, 65, 67, 77

S

Sacred Geometry, 138

Savannah Hypothesis, 17

Scale, 31, 61, 94, 95, 155, 158, 181

Schematic design, 125, 131, 174

Scientific studies, 15, 21, 53

Seaming technologies, 68, 129

Seating group, 37, 83, 98, 122

Senior-living facilities, 38, 48, 58

Shadows, 73-75

Shamanism, 23

Shapes, 110, 116, 121-23, 130, 132, 171, 177

Shea Labagh Dobberstein, 41

Shifting energy, 30

Sidewalks, 31, 61, 62, 115

Slippery, 6, 25, 182

Solid-colors, 136, 155, 176

Square, 103, 129, 137

Squint Test, 6, 59, 77, 95, 145

Staff, 11, 32, 37, 41-42, 66, 85, 100, 119, 138, 142-45, 161-62, 172, 181-182, 188

Stairs, 48, 96

Starchitect, 33

Stone, 29, 31, 61, 80, 111, 156, 160, 169, 171, 176, 180

Strategy, 58, 62, 75, 112, 121-23, 126, 183

Streetscape, 31

Stress, 6, 8-9, 26, 39, 41-42, 45, 55, 63, 83, 89, 93, 97, 101, 141, 153, 157-159, 161, 169, 175

Stripes, 65-66, 95-96, 102, 121-23, 144-45, 157

Structure, 56, 75, 160

Sun angles, 74

Supermarket, 75, 108

Surfaces, 47-48, 61, 78, 130, 155, 174, 178

Sustainable, 13, 188

Symmetrical border, 80

Symmetry, 102, 128, 136, 160

T

Table, 65-67, 87, 100

Terrazzo, 120, 125

Tertiary care hospital, 85,119

Texture, 39, 57, 80, 94, 96, 110, 131, 136, 150, 157, 170, 173, 180

The New York Times, 172

The Vital Spirit, 90

Tile, 35, 41, 77, 79, 80, 86, 95, 111, 114, 128, 136, 143-44, 150, 158, 172-75, 180-81

T-intersection, 92

Toddler, 62

Touch, 91, 169

Traditional, 29, 32, 38

Traditions, 18, 35

Transition, 28-31, 65, 67-69, 78

Transportation projects, 56, 112

Tripping and falling, 6-7, 22, 65

U

Ungud, 90, 147

V

Value engineering, 57
Vastu Shastra, 18-19, 20
VCT, 80, 128
Vedic, 20, 38, 102
Vinyl, 7, 66-69, 80, 111, 125, 129, 175, 178
Vision-impaired, 24, 58, 74, 76, 78, 81, 123
Visualizing, 33

W

Waiting Room, 112, 121, 124
Walkways, 73, 107, *See also Pathways*
Walls, 46, 48-59, 73, 78, 82, 86, 125, 178, 180
Warm Colors, 136, 151, 162

Wayfinding, 85-86, 111, 119-133
Wild Planet Toys, 149-50
Wind tunnel, 89-103
Winding riverbank, 85, 112
Winding roads, 105
Wood, 39, 86, 148, 158, 169-71, 175, 177-78, 180
Workplaces, 34, 58, 147
Workstations, 49, 85, 100, 113, 142-143, 149, 150

Y

Yellow tinting of the eye, 154
Yin and Yang, 135-164
Yin/Yang Energy Charts, 136-37

Z

Zoologist, 167
Zoos, 168

ABOUT THE AUTHOR

Barbara Lyons Stewart is an Architect, Interior Designer, Consultant, Speaker and Author with a specialty in both Ancient and Modern Forms of Environmental Psychology, ranging from Feng Shui to Evidence Based Design. She has spent more than 25 years helping clients including Kaiser Permanente, KGO/ABC Television, Wild Planet Toys, The Republic of Tea, KTVU Fox/Cox Media and The New York Times with her firm Lyons Stewart Architects and as a Consultant on large project teams. Her office is located in the San Francisco Bay Area.

Barbara's speaking engagements include three National AIA Conventions, the 2012 IIDA SoCal Speaker Series, the 2011 Healthcare Design Conference and many architectural and interior design firms.

For information about planned upcoming books, resources and a full biography and client list, please visit her websites www.LyonsArch.com and www. ArchitecturalDesignPsychology. com.

To contact Barbara about Speaking, Training Workshops and Consulting to benefit your own architectural or interior design firm; your flooring manufacturing, marketing or sales organization; or your own business in any project type, please e-mail: Barbara @ LyonsArch.com.

The Publisher and Author make no representations or warranties with respect to the accuracy and completeness of the contents of this work and specifically disclaim all warranties, including without limitation warranties of fitness of information and recommendations included in this book for a particular purpose, project type, facility or client. The advice and strategies contained herein describe one design approach for helping to avoid some of the physical and psychological issues and problems related to flooring selection and design, and should be combined with industry-standard flooring strategies and methodologies relating to flooring materials, patterns and design to achieve the best results for end-users. The strategies described in this book may not be suitable for every situation. This work is sold with the understanding that the Author is not rendering any professional services by writing, selling or distributing this book.

If professional assistance is required, then the services of a competent professional person should be sought. Neither the Publisher nor the Author shall be liable for damages arising herefrom and based upon the information included in this book. The fact that an individual, organization, reference or website is referred to in this work as a citation and/or existing or potential source of information does not mean that the Author or Publisher endorses the information those sources may provide or recommendations they may make. Further, readers should be aware that internet websites listed in this work may have changed or disappeared between when this work was written and when it was read.

www.ingramcontent.com/pod-product-compliance
Lightning Source LLC
Chambersburg PA
CBHW071715160426
43195CB00012B/1692